Anonymous No More

Anonymous
No More

ONE MOTHER'S FAITH-FILLED JOURNEY
THROUGH ADDICTION, RECOVERY
& REDEMPTION

ALISA MASSEY

NEW YORK

Anonymous No More

ONE MOTHER'S FAITH-FILLED JOURNEY THROUGH ADDICTION, RECOVERY & REDEMPTION

Published in New York, New York, by Morgan James Publishing. Morgan James and The Entrepreneurial Publisher are trademarks of Morgan James, LLC. www.MorganJamesPublishing.com

The Morgan James Speakers Group can bring authors to your live event. For more information or to book an event visit The Morgan James Speakers Group at www.TheMorganJamesSpeakersGroup.com.

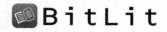

A FREE eBook edition is available with the purchase of this print book

CLEARLY PRINT YOUR NAME IN THE BOX ABOVE

Instructions to claim your free eBook edition:
1. Download the BitLit app for Android or iOS
2. Write your name in UPPER CASE in the box
3. Use the BitLit app to submit a photo
4. Download your eBook to any device

ISBN 978-1-63047-285-6 paperback
ISBN 978-1-63047-286-3 eBook
ISBN 978-1-63047-287-0 hardcover
Library of Congress Control Number: 2014941192

Cover Design by:
Rachel Lopez
www.r2cdesign.com

Interior Design by:
Bonnie Bushman
bonnie@caboodlegraphics.com

In an effort to support local communities, raise awareness and funds, Morgan James Publishing donates a percentage of all book sales for the life of each book to Habitat for Humanity Peninsula and Greater Williamsburg.

Get involved today, visit
www.MorganJamesBuilds.com.

Habitat
for Humanity®
Peninsula and
Greater Williamsburg
Building Partner

In loving memory of my mother Paula Lee Wilcox
September 2, 1952–September 7, 2006

This book is dedicated to the suffering addict.
And to Van's House…thanks for all you do!

Table of Contents

Preface

For eight long years, I was deeply impacted by the ferocious disease of alcohol and drug addiction. I lost out on countless opportunities and immeasurable joy. Most of all, I lost out on my kids. Those special little moments of tiny fingers and toes were replaced by empty photo books for a period of time as alcohol and drugs entrenched themselves in my mind, body, and soul. As a result of my actions, my time with my children was deeply impacted. But my story doesn't end there. God showed me that I didn't have to be forever chained up by my past afflictions. A new song and dance now play a blossoming melody in my life. The chains of wrath could not hold me hostage forever.

Through many different circumstances, God uses special people to guide us back to the right direction. But we must want and accept that help. We must cry out for it. Sometimes that shout for help happens just in the nick of time—other times, it comes too late. But if we can reach out and share our stories of hope and redemption with others who are hurting, perhaps their cries will turn to tears of joy. Hopefully, there are many lost souls who can still be reached. And just maybe, addiction's captives can be set free.

Alcohol is an insidious disease—make no mistake of that. Too many are unaware of alcohol's sting. Perhaps they don't realize or they are in denial of the rising issue; or maybe they are aware of their transgression, but they're unsure of where to turn or whom to call. Many of its victims have families, including children. Their stories are not always widely heard. This is why I wanted to share my story. Many times in the sober house, I yearned to hear stories similar to my own. To find someone I could relate with, someone who could give me encouragement and hope because I so thirsted for change. The concept that we all desire better for our lives has reinvigorated me to boldly stand up and provide hope to those who crave it. And to share God's grace.

Writing this book has also helped me continue my own healing, and it's opened my eyes to boundless joy. Like with anything, the beginning was tough, but the way got easier with time, and eventually I reached a remarkably happy ending. And this can be your ending, too, alcoholic or not. All you need is God! With Him we are safe, and happy endings are boundless—even in death. There is everlasting life because God redeems.

Acknowledgments

First and foremost, I would like to thank our Creator God and His only son, Jesus Christ. Thank you for showing me how to live.

I would like to thank my father, Frank Humphries, for having faith in all I do, and for the numerous times you never gave up on me.

I wholeheartedly thank Scott and Sally Van Krevelen for saving my life. Thank you for providing hope and a home for countless alcoholics and addicts.

Thank you to my husband, Dusty, for unconditionally loving me and never giving up on our family. I love you.

Thank you to our awesome children for all your love and endless smiles.

Thanks to my sponsor, Jeanie, for helping me through the steps and for being so wonderful!

Thanks to Aunt Linda, Grandma, Brenda, Amy, my two older brothers Derrick and Chad, and the rest of my family and friends for all your love and support. You are greatly appreciated!

A special thank you to Morgan James Publishing for believing in me.

And last but not least, I want to thank my mother who is now in heaven. I'm excited to reunite with you in the clouds some day!

Please Note:
Some names have been changed
to protect privacy.

Introduction

As infants, we are pure and free. We glisten and shine, having just exited from heavenly realms up above. As children, we find ourselves growing up in a sinful, unforgiving world. We learn habits, we follow those around us, and we make our choices.

In the beginning, I was an innocent, sweet, brown-eyed, brown-haired little girl. As I grew, I found my vices. First, I was influenced by sin from family and friends—anyone with an influence in my life. Before long, sin enticed me, gripping my throat and leaving me gasping for breath. The ultimate sin that would leave me defenseless brought me to my knees. Unless an act of God could save me, I would die. My innocence had all but dissipated.

I would soon be reassured there was, indeed, escape from sin; but its effects were inescapable. The aftermath of my sin sent me into a tailspin.

Alcohol and drugs became my greatest demons. I can't say my greatest sin, because no one sin is worse than any other. Sin is sin. It is true, however, that there are different consequences to our sin. The damage caused by my sin was severe but not completely irreparable. I lost everything because of my addiction to drugs and alcohol. Most importantly, what I treasure most in this life was taken away from me.

Only divine guidance could pull me out of this sin.

It may sound odd, but truth resides at the crossroads. When I could no longer live with my actions or the consequences thereof, I decided that I was done with alcohol and drugs. But I couldn't do this alone. I cried out to our Maker at just the right time. And that's when God said, "She's ready now."

Although I thought losing everything was the end, I was truly mistaken. Instead, it was another great beginning—the start of an intimate relationship with a loving God. Life became better than it had ever been before my disaster struck. My trust in God deepened through affliction. I now appreciate life. And with that life, the sweetness of the rose has infused my soul, overriding the poison. Now I can be a vessel for God, helping others (addict or not) through the words of this book and in many other ways. I am now a living testimony to God's grace. Significantly, my children can have the best of me.

Thank God, I have been redeemed. God has restored my innocence. Nothing can break me now, not even addiction.

CHAPTER 1

The Bad Gene

The year was 1985. Mom, Dad, me, and my older two brothers Chad and Derrick packed in tight in front of Grandma's fireplace for a family photo. Back then, we appeared a normal family as far as the eye could see. The trouble with this "normalcy" is that it was superficial. People can look pretty and neat on the outside, but on the inside it may be a complete different story. Little did our family know, this seemingly perfect image would soon be torn jaggedly apart. Events to come would rip through each of us. One by one, we would each face our own trials, and in one way or the other, we would each be harshly affected by one major culprit that lurked within us.

D rinking was in the blood. But this didn't sink in until its stain afflicted me. At first, the stain was faint, but after a while the bleeding would not stop. And at first, I didn't fit the profile. I was a cheerleader and a stellar student; a teacher's pet at times. My father drank Crown Royal but always managed it. My mother didn't drink in her humble beginnings. But things would change. At some point, I became aware of half-empty bottles stashed in bathroom cabinets and began witnessing outlandish mood swings from Mom. I guess no matter how you put it, for some who are bitten by this ferocious disease, it's tough to suck out the poison, and scars often remain. Some are deeper than others, and some remain hidden.

I was six years old when Mom and Dad divorced. Divorce seems commonplace in today's broken world, and happy endings seldom follow. My siblings and I were all impacted by our parent's divorce. Rumors circulated of how Dad drank plentifully after the split. They say he had a tough time, that he was deeply depressed and hid out for a while. True or not, things slowly got better for him. Life went on eventually. My mother became the hard case. Although she moved on and remarried, a chain of events soon occurred that would forever change who she was, making it tough to pinpoint the catalyst of her change.

Most people would call my mom beautiful. Luxurious, long, blond hair. Bright, shiny blue eyes surrounded with dark, thick lashes. She was homecoming queen for the class of '69 at Tonkawa High. She wore the title well and resembled Brigitte Bardot. But she stood out for another reason. Even more distinguishable about her was the beautiful person who resided within. Satisfyingly sweet, giving, and big-hearted—with every inch of her small frame, she loved graciously. She was truly an angel. And Dad thought so too. So, in 1970, he married his high-school sweetheart. They had a shotgun wedding and had three children together thereafter, each five years apart. Derrick, Chad, and myself.

Dad, mom, Derrick, Chad,
and me, Christmas 1985.

Me at 5-years-old.

Dancing days.

Mom was artistic, too. She painted spectacular landscapes, representative of God's great earth. Old-fashioned barns lying in green, spacious pastures of the countryside, trees speckled in soft colors of the fall, all blended together perfectly by her smooth, angelic hand at the brush. While she looked like an angel, she received her wings and soared high when she was fast at work on her canvas. Her paintings brought life to crisp autumn or snowcapped mountains in the dead of winter. She loved to paint God's naturalistic scenery in all its splendor. The paintings were as much a part of her as words are to a writer or a tune to a songwriter. Her art completed her, and God revealed Himself through these beautiful paintings, just as He did through her soft, delicate features and kindhearted soul. God's presence embraced her as He does us all, but her work and her beauty made it so obvious to the naked eye.

But life wouldn't always be easy for her. One cold, dreary morning, Mom ventured out on her twenty-mile drive to work. It had snowed steadily the day before, and the roadways were not completely clear. Suddenly, as she crossed a bridge in her yellow, two-door Mustang convertible, she hit a patch of black ice. She lost control of the compact car, and it flew off the side of the overpass, tumbling seventeen feet to the ground below. The crushed car landed right-side-up with the soft top caved in, leaving Mom stranded in the jumbled wreckage. Rescue personnel had to use the Jaws of Life to free her shambled body.

Mom's best friend Vicki quickly came to my first-grade classroom at Washington Elementary. She cut to the chase. "Sweetie, your mom's been in a car wreck." How else do you break the news to a six-year-old? That is all I remember of that terrifying moment. The only thing more frightening was seeing her bruised, broken body in the dark, cold ICU room. I placed my tiny fingers around her bloodstained hands, and she squeezed my hand as best she could. I hoped, of course, that Mom would be okay. Sadly, things never seemed to be the same again. Not only for her, but for all of us.

Recovery progressed slowly as expected for someone in her condition. The accident wreaked havoc on her back and neck, and she sported a back brace for a year thereafter. The year of the accident was the same year Mom and Dad got divorced. Even still, life progressed, and Mom found herself knee-deep in love again with a pilot named George. Mom and George got married, and I lived with them. George started out flying small airplanes in Ponca City, Oklahoma. He was tall, dark, and handsome. Those features only masked the demons that eventually made their way out.

The abuse came out of nowhere—completely unexpected. Like a raging bull, he stampeded through our lives, making it hard to recall any good from my childhood. Abuse is indeed a powerful element, and I learned a lot from that time in our lives. Images of George relentlessly beating my mother—and her fighting back the best she knew how—remained fresh in my mind for a long time. I have since chosen to block out those stark images. They are of no use to me anymore; I revisit them only in an effort to help someone else.

When I was eleven years old, George got a job with Continental Airlines and was transferred to Oahu, Hawaii. Although the abuse hadn't stopped, Mom and I moved with him. My brothers remained with Dad in our hometown, Tonkawa, Oklahoma.

Now we were stuck with the violent attacks, miles away from home. We were essentially deserted on an island with no place to escape. The cycle of George's abuse continued. We lived in Aiea, Hawaii, in a pink apartment complex. It was very pretty on the outside, but that was overshadowed by the ugliness inside apartment 306. Loud screaming matches shook the building. One particular day, I broke down. I couldn't take the fighting anymore. But there was nowhere to turn but up.

I buried my head in my tear-soaked pillow and cried out to God. "Please, please, make it stop! Help us, God!" Although the situation did not get instantly better, I knew He was with me. And He carried me through that moment.

That summer George's son Tom came to visit. Tom and I stood in the living room, listening to George banging Mom's head up against the shower. She was screaming frantically. Tom began to laugh. I was now just as disturbed about him as I was his dad. So many times through that summer, I tried reaching for the phone, but George instantly threatened me. Finally during one episode, I did call the cops, but George slammed down the phone. They came later that day, but Mom told me to tell them everything was fine. Mom's drinking became obvious somewhere around this time. I went to third grade in Hawaii for almost a whole year before we returned home to Oklahoma.

How or why, God only knows, but two summers later, Mom and I were off to the Big Island again, this time without George. Nonetheless, trouble still lurked around every corner as we were often without a home and without money. I recall Mom drinking and acting crazy this time. What had become of her? Was the car wreck to blame for all this outlandish behavior? Or was it the abuse? Perhaps it was a combination of the two? I don't know, but one thing is for sure: The alcohol only hastened her demise.

As we left for Hawaii that summer, Dad mourned my departure. It was a bright, sunshiny day outside, but inwardly our hearts were pouring rain. Grandma picked me up at Dad's house in Tonkawa to take me to the Tulsa airport. As I loaded my belongings in the car, Dad put his head up against the Buick LeSabre and began to cry. Once again, his little girl was leaving him to reside so far away. That was the first time I ever saw him shed a tear.

Part of that summer, Mom and I lived with a guy named Roberto. We came and went from that house frequently. He was an odd duck. One evening, as darkness invaded the house, I crept toward the kitchen, only to find Mom sitting on a chair in the middle of the living room, her pretty head tilted back with a bottle to her lips. She was chugging. Something was obviously wrong. But I never knew specifics—perhaps I wouldn't have understood. I did know, however, that I wanted to go home to Dad's, in Oklahoma. I hadn't even talked to Dad for the whole summer. Then, finally it was a few days before school started, and he called out to Hawaii to ask if I was coming home. I was happy when my return was arranged.

Threats of a hurricane on the island stalled my flight home, but the threat quickly dissipated, and I was on my way. I arrived back home to Tonkawa one day late for sixth grade—but I made it! My second day of school, I was still shook up from the whole frightening experience. Friends remarked, "I bet that was nice getting to live in Hawaii for the whole summer." I remember thinking quite the opposite! But I kept my mouth shut. Who would understand?

After Hawaii and throughout my teen years, I lived with Dad in Tonkawa. Mom continued to move around a lot, and after my junior year of high school, she vanished altogether; our family couldn't find her. That part of her life remains a mystery, and that's the way it's meant to be. Mom was fighting her own battles. She re-occurred at my high school graduation, though. She would win the battle in the end, but not the way we expected. She won the way that God wanted; and God knows best. He wanted to take her out of the pain she was in, to a better place. I only wished that I could have been more help to her. I will always remember the time Mom and I shared in Hawaii, although it wasn't always the best of circumstances. For a brief moment in time, we connected.

I share with you this part of my story to show how drinking can be a family affair in addition to being a disease. I hope to help you understand that, to everybody's story, there just might be a reasoning for how they behave. It's called "learned behavior." The solution is that we simply need to educate each other. We must be aware that our actions greatly affect others, especially our children. The wreckage of abuse, drugs, and alcohol can cripple children and loved ones for years. I am living proof of that. But I am also here to proclaim that life goes on! And it can get better! I could not imagine back then ever living fearlessly, or even being happy, for that matter.

I love my mom. She was a beauty, inside and out. Why that set of circumstances happened to her, I'll never know. Like with many of life's curveballs, it's not meant for me to understand. But I can learn from it. What misery she must have been facing while here on earth. Who knew I would be next in line to face the same misery that brought her down from what she once was. My older brothers were consumed by alcohol and drugs as well. One by one, the drinking took us all down. But for all of my siblings, that same misery would be our greatest blessing, and we would recover. And ultimately, Mom had it better than us—she escaped it all and moved to heaven.

Mom died in 2006, from cancer. Her body could no longer withstand this cruel earth. There were better things in store for her up above. A better place awaited her in heaven, and she was ready. Now she could be happy again. And for that, I am happy. Her words still ring true to me today: "Dreams are what we're made of, and I'm working on yours." Indeed, she is.

CHAPTER 2

A Social Affair

In high school, I was determined to be my best. Being exposed to violence and a missing mother throughout my teen years had made me tough. I did not feel the need to rebel at first; rather I felt the need to excel. I would stay in my room many nights studying exhaustively for tests. Journaling, writing—soaking in anything to further advance myself. My major downfall was my need to please others. I liked people and wanted to please them. I tried to make everyone happy, at my own expense. I had no boundaries, and I was yet unaware of my acquired alcoholic gene. In my life, my family, my hometown, alcohol was accepted and overlooked as any potential life-threatening illness. But I was specifically chosen by God for a unique position. In the end, the Almighty One is glorified. And at our life's conclusion, that is all that matters. The devil may use alcohol and drugs as deadly weapons, but God is greater.

My first drink consisted of a wine cooler. Harmless, you might think. But the simple act of drinking that wine cooler would prove the killer. I was easily deceived by the need to fit in, a common problem of many teenagers. I fell prey to curiosity, peer pressure, the need to feel accepted. But I was the odd duck. I had a gene just waiting to bud. All it needed was a little feeding. Still unaware that I had acquired this gene, I went on tempting the poisonous snake. It soon spat its venom at me and reached out earnestly for its prey; it would stop at nothing to possess me. From then on out, the only effective source of help would come from God Himself, at which point the master plan would be revealed.

Witnessing violence and abuse as an adolescent forced me to grow up early; my innocence was destroyed. This could have worked to my benefit—but when it came to peer pressure, I gave in every time. The older crowd intrigued me, and I was introduced to new adventures such as booze cruising. I soon became another face in this unruly crowd. At the time, I thought the escapades were harmless. But my desire to please people was soon overshadowed by my need to feed the hunger. Twelve-packs of Bud Light became thirty-packs; dirt roads became an escape to ease my weary mind. Cruising intently down the sandy roads, we would blare our favorite Def Leppard tune, chugging beer after beer and singing at the top of our lungs; "Pour some sugar on me!" But when it rains, it pours; and these old tracks would soon become covered in mud and cracked beyond repair.

Cheerleading 1998

Mom and me at my Junior prom, 1998.

And so the party continued. As a high-school cheerleader my junior year, I became a regular partygoer. I cared more about the bottle than boys. Awkwardly shy at first, I entered the room with my black miniskirt and long, brown hair, beer bottle in hand. I was ready to blend in with the others, so the tippling began. After a few toddies, the shyness dissipated. I was now suited up with confidence. But it was a fake sense of confidence, blanketing the miles of insecurity road mapped inside. Soon life's big party replaced extracurricular activities and began taking precedence over everything. And the great fall began.

Despite many wild nights with the drinking crew, my life and my license were spared. After a while, I could handle my own—in other words, I could drink a load of booze. In one instance, my best friend Carrie and I stopped on a dirt road to finish off our gallon of Jose Cuervo. We had Aerosmith cranked up and oozing out the windows. Steven Tyler was singing, "Crazy." There couldn't have been a better song to fit the moment. We managed to finish off the Cuervo, and then I went blank. I blacked out. My last recollection was flipping cartwheels across the dirt road, assuredly falling on my face. Petite Carrie carried me into her grandmother's house.

"You threw up in your sleep; I turned you over," was the first thing Carrie said when I woke up. "I told Grandma you ate something bad," she went on. If Grandma would have known how bad, how dangerous some of these drunken splurges were, perhaps the pursuit of recovery would have started much earlier. Sadly however, for many alcoholics and addicts, the pursuit of recovery never occurs because the need for help is never exposed. Some hide it. Others are unsure it's a problem. Others, family included, are in denial. And some enjoy sugarcoating. The lucky ones who escape death may only wake up when they hit the bottom. Although everybody's bottom is different, it is in this pit where many victims finally cry out. Their plea for help and perhaps their desire to quit is the strongest, the most elevated at that point. I would soon reside in this dark place, but I would first travel though many more diverted paths. And although the decisions I made were my own, these mind-altered thoughts were highly encouraged by a deep, dark side that came out to play with just a single thirst of alcohol.

I still have dreams that haunt me of the terror left behind.

Anxiety was definitely another one of my demons. I was strong enough then to withstand impure thoughts; I could send them back to the raging fires below. I remember that first anxiety attack—the feeling as my heart began to race and my palms grew sweaty against my pencil. "You have ten minutes to finish your test," said Mrs. Mulger, my ninth-grade math teacher. Math was my weakness, and so were the tests. The dread made my heart race faster. I bent over to tie my shoestring, attempting to distract myself from the strong palpations beating against my chest. That distraction did minimize what was physically occurring. The attack was brief, and I could revert back to functioning normally; back to my test. No breakdown. No trauma just yet.

I made a good grade on the test, but anxiety attacks became a common event for me. The minor attacks were enough to get my blood flowing. At times they gave me the adrenaline I needed to get moving. They were harmless, yet enough to leave a taste of fear in my mouth, a sour taste I didn't care to experience again. For years, I maintained a semblance of control, but once I added alcohol to the mix, I could no longer withstand the anxiety. As powerful as those early anxiety attacks were, they were minor in comparison to the full-fledged attacks that would soon thrust their way through my mind, body, and soul. The more I drank, the more the anxiety escalated, exploding in my body like a scientific experiment gone wrong, the fuming gases infecting my body.

Many more nights of drunken stupor continued through my junior and senior years. Endless nights of drinking and driving, playing beer pong, drunken card games, acting stupid, and getting sick. These occurrences were overlooked every time. Drinking was something the majority of kids in our area did, and it was downplayed by the adults around us. Even a couple of drinking and driving accidents leading to deaths in Tonkawa were not enough to encourage an end to the cycle. For some, it became a reason to drink more. "I drink this fine Budweiser in honor of Johnny Cane," they would say. They seemed to be missing the message, and many still do. It's a tough battle between heaven and hell, this alcohol and drug problem, and many find out too late just how badly a person can be burned by its flame. The glory of it all, though, is that I have lived to tell about it, to help the next person because—finally—I got it.

Despite the high life in high school, I managed to graduate salutatorian. I had not yet lost the will to succeed. My drive and my strong study habits had not yet dissipated. I was at the top of my class because I worked the hardest, not because I was the smartest. A few key people in my life—dad's sister, Aunt Janis (she passed away in 2001) and my dad—continued to encourage me to study hard and insisted that I must go to college if I wanted to make anything of my life. Little did they know I needed to be encouraged to not drink as well. I needed to be encouraged to be different from the pack; to stand alone so I wouldn't be swept away by bad influences. I needed to learn to hold my ground. Deep down inside, I desired something more than what the crowd had to offer. It's amazing how just a small dose of poison can drastically turn a person off the track God intended them to be on. I know, because that's what happened to me.

I quit cheerleading my senior year to "move on the other things." I still enjoyed dancing and cheering, but I no longer was interested in high-school stuff. I had other things in mind. I wanted to earn a dollar and survive on my own. This desire stemmed from that longing of wanting to be somebody. Despite family members' stories of how they coulda, woulda, shoulda, and despite knowing firsthand of family members who were also stained by the unwanted effects of alcohol, my determination to move forward and upward soon became buried in the ground. My addiction came out of nowhere, it called my name, tempted me, and begged me to cave in, until one day I just wanted a taste. And that's all it took.

I started my first job at Milly's Bar and Grill at the end of my senior year, spring semester of 1999. I was an awesome waitress with a strong work ethic. I worked well with customers and acquired many favorites. They enjoyed me too; some regularly requested me as their waitress. It made me feel good to know that I had graduated high school well and that people thought I was an exceptional waitress. I was making good money, too, and I soon could afford my own little one-bedroom duplex. Once I turned twenty-one, I was promoted to assistant manager/bartender. I was an excellent bartender, but bartending was not good to me. The temptation was always present as I popped bottle after bottle and poured stout drinks. I poured them just as I would have liked them. That atmosphere was deadly for me; it fed my desire for drink even more. I was living at a feverish pace. We would all look forward to closing time, when it was our turn to tap the keg. My mouth would be watering by this point. Often that just got me started. When I stumbled out the door at one o'clock in the morning, I would head straight to the nearest Conoco for a twelve-pack—that is, if I didn't have plans for the Rocking Horse, the local honky-tonk. I would find all the town's local faves at this joint, and we'd let loose with a few longnecks, and close down the bar every time.

Meanwhile, college had started out smoothly, and the road appeared promising. But just like the bartending, it soon ended in disaster—a spiraling tornado, leaving behind miles of destruction. I began by majoring in communications with dreams of being a TV reporter. I did very well in my classes, especially speech and English. Writing was my strongest asset, and it was at Northern Oklahoma College I began writing my first news stories. In the beginning, straight As were a signature grade for me. I was even a DJ on the radio for 90.7, The Source. I was entirely enthusiastic about that kind of stuff and had the grades to prove it. Math was my weakness, but I still maintained a solid B. But alcohol soon made its imprint on all educational endeavors as well. I didn't graduate with my associate degree in communications until December of 2005. My grade point dropped several notches from my original 4.0, because I managed to receive an F in English for skipping out on class. I couldn't make it out of bed. Hangovers were all too frequent.

Soon anxiety dominated every inch of me. I became fearful of crowds, of riding in vehicles, fearful of stepping foot in a shopping mall. I even avoided talking on the phone. I needed a drink to talk on the phone! Once a communications major, I could no longer communicate, period. Nor did I want to, and leaving the house was a chore. No matter where the anxiety stemmed from—the alcohol, the withdrawal, increasing fear—it became a primer to consume more at an alarming rate. Even during those periods of my life that I didn't drink, the attacks still came like arrows headed straight for the bulls-eye, with me as the target every time. The fear would not subside; it would paralyze me temporarily. Sleep became a rare thing unless I drank myself to bed. I was afraid to wake up, fearing the unknown once again—yet I was terrified I would not wake up at all. Thanks to alcohol, my world had become the unknown.

I was with my Aunt Linda in the car one time when the terror struck at me again. Like a raging, mad bull, it charged straight toward me, aiming to run me over, physically and mentally. We drove the speed limit from Tonkawa to Tulsa, two-and-a-half hours of freaking out with nowhere to escape. After all, it's not like I could jump out of a moving vehicle the way I envisioned doing in my feeble mind. All the while, silence resided. Inside, my brain was going haywire; electrically convulsed by me. Aunt Linda sensed something was wrong but said nothing. Occasionally she tried making conversation, but I was not capable of any normal interaction. I just knew she was going to say something about my odd behavior, but she never did. And I was glad. I didn't want to talk about it. But keeping quiet was never the best remedy. I was putting Band-Aids over my problems, then ripping them off before the wounds properly healed. But God desired to heal my wounds the proper way. He had the perfect plan. Part of this plan was for me to search and find where the root of the problem thrived. I needed to discover my identity through God's eyes, but first I had to admit defeat.

My duplex on Seventh Street became my escape from a world I no longer wanted to face. At times, I refrained from answering the phone or door. Often, I experienced horrible anxiety attacks on the way home from work. To ease my poisoned body of the anxiety that coursed through it, I would chug one drink after the other until I finally reached my destination. I could breathe better once I reached my little place of seclusion. There, I was safe from the roads and the rest of society. But before pulling into seclusion, I had to make sure the fridge was stocked. This was my safety net. It soon became a challenge to make it in and out of the store. I was now completely riveted by fear. Chewing my stale gum to ease my nerves, I would feverishly enter the store, avoiding all eye contact. I was on a mission.

In one strange, desperate quest for beer, I walked down to the convenience store in camouflage and black army boots. Reaching into the cooler, I pulled out a twelve-pack of Bud Light bottles. "It sure is a cold morning to be going hunting," I told the store owner. That time, there were no raised eyebrows. Often my sense of kindness helped people to overlook my major defect for destruction. They weren't aware of my problem; therefore, they did not judge me just yet. That time would come soon enough.

Three years later, my job at Milly's Bar and Grill came to an end. I could no longer support my habit at work, so I quit. One bill after the other began to stack up. Dragging myself in to work each sorrowful day became too much of a chore for my alcohol-drenched body full of bubbling drink from the night before. Therefore, I wouldn't work. As it was, no sooner than I would arrive at Milly's to work, my mind would stampede in a panicking fit; it couldn't grasp the thought of doing without.

A domino effect would then force my body into a full-blown panic attack. I had to hide in seclusion, I decided. Away from work. This struggle had become too much for me. And shameful acts such as this one caused me to drink more. I was disgusted with myself. What would I do now?

One cold, wintery morning, I awoke to see my breath as I breathed in and out, my mouth stinking of stale beer. My gas had been shut off. But like with anything else at this point, I no longer cared. As long as I had a Bud Light to warm my body, I would be okay—or so I thought. Next up for my humiliation was my '99 black Trans Am Ram Air. It was another chilly morning when I heard the sounds of metal against metal. I couldn't look, because I knew what was about to occur. I hadn't made my five-hundred-dollar payment in over four months, and the old black bird was now repossessed.

Amid all the late night partying, I became pregnant with Jayden. Once I realized I was pregnant, I stopped the drinking and drugs, but this was much more difficult than I expected. That should have been the first piece of evidence suggesting I was hooked; nonetheless, I ignored the signs. By the grace of God, I managed to get off the booze and pills. But Jayden was born on August 3, 2004, and very soon after, I miserably found my way back to the bottle. I was in desperation mode, only now I was dragging my precious child along for the long haul, too. Now a single mother living with her father, I continually lost my battles with drugs and alcohol.

The guilt I endured for not managing responsibility made me desire more bubbly. But since I was no longer working, I had to try something new. I attempted college once more. I went on to attend Oklahoma State University. Jayden was two. I would drop him off at daycare, travel an hour to get to class, and then at night I would try to study. Somehow, I always found time or an excuse to fit in a stiff drink. After all, I did have a habit to maintain. Sometimes I would even buy a six-pack after class for the long ride home from school, especially on days when I had increased anxiety. As long as sedatives were present to calm my frazzled nerves, I could survive in my sea of constant chaos. Drinking went hand in hand with studying, just like it did with everything else.

Before long, sitting in class became increasingly difficult. My body constantly felt as if a shock wave were consuming it. This sensation overtook any remaining ability to concentrate, until one day in 2006, in biology class at Oklahoma State University, I broke. I sat there, trying to focus. My hands began to sweat. It was a tight fit in there. My elbows rubbed up against my neighbors', startling me into a social anxiety fit. Next came those strong palpitations. A slow, awkward pace at first, but the beats grew quicker in pace.

I could feel an explosion coming on. All the bleak possibilities raced through my head. I would pass out any minute, I thought. They would call the ambulance. Or maybe I could softly drift out, not making a peep. Unnoticed. Or maybe, all eyes on me, I would make a mad dash. People must have thought I was crazy. I opted for the mad dash to my Honda Civic and rushed to the Conoco for a six-pack— but first I had to swallow a Xanax for the anxiety fit that electrified my body. A couple of pink-colored pills were my only instant relief.

I was ashamed, and I got to a point where I no longer wanted to face my classmates; it seemed easier just to ignore the problems. After all, ignoring them was what I had been doing most all my life. But then I would try again. Over and over—it became an escalating cycle until I could no longer meet the demands of college. Instead, I continued to feed my body those toxins, avoiding the panicky rage from lack thereof. I feared the panic attacks worse than anything.

The party never stopped, but my period did again. Four years after Jayden was born, I was pregnant with another child. Annie was born January 26, 2009. Jayden and Annie's dad's name was Bill, and he and I were not together throughout my pregnancy or after Annie was born. I again refrained from alcohol and drugs throughout my pregnancy. But shortly after Annie's birth, Carrie came along, knocking at my door with a bottle of White Zinfandel. I had a lot of catching up to do as far as drinking was concerned. The wine looked pretty and pink, and my mouth quickly began to water. I thought nothing of it at the time as I grabbed a wine glass out of the cabinet and poured some to the rim. We toasted to "new life"—it seemed the perfect excuse to drink the whole bottle and then get more. More often than not, I found every excuse to drink alcohol whether it be celebrating a special occasion or basking in sadness. After Annie was born, I was still unaware I needed rehab, or even that I had a problem. I was blinded by my sin. I had yet to learn that addiction was more than just getting off alcohol and drugs, it was about recognizing and learning to deal with defects of character, such as insecurity, anger, and resentment.

Mom's death from cancer sent me deep into despair. Despite the arrival of my two beautiful children that should have changed my path for the better, I eventually gave up on school and began drinking and drugging full time. I offered the world empty promises and sweet nothings. For the next two years, life was a blur. The mixtures of alcohol and other drugs such as Xanax and cocaine swallowed me into a long, lost trance. Something had to give.

My face had become pale and expressionless, my body— hands, feet, stomach, face—was all puffed up from excess alcohol. At this point I should have been in detox, heavily monitored so as not to go into convulsions. The brain that had won me the title of most studious in high school had disappeared some time ago in the midst of a drunk tank. It would require lots of time and effort to restore back to normal.

CHAPTER 3

Breaking Point

We all deserve a second chance, but this doesn't mean we will get it. If and when a chance for change comes along, it's what we do with that opportunity that will determine our outcome. One major issue for promoting change for the better is that some people are not aware that opportunity is available or where to find it. More, if they are aware, they are scared to take the leap of faith required to achieve this better life. People who are in a broken state such as I was often require encouragement and a desire for hope. Sadly, the encouragement is not always there until something bad happens, and it is only then the need for change gets through.

I n the summer of 2009, I ignored a significant warning sign in my draw to alcohol. Jayden was four and Annie five months. It was a beautiful summer day, and I decided to take Jayden and Annie to our family's farm, down one of the many dirt roads I had traveled on with friends for booze cruising as a teen. I wasn't booze cruising on this day, however. Like every other day at that time, I had already started my daily fix of alcohol. I'd had two drinks prior to our trip. But there were times I drank more with Jayden in the car. Whether the alcohol on that day played a part or not, I recall my gray HHR leaving the road. I can see it in slow motion—we were upside down, then right-side-up again. All of us were untouched by the roll. The car was not so lucky. The back glass shattered to bits, and the top caved in but not enough to hurt us. God was with us, for sure. It was just one of the many times He would protect us.

My second chances were running out. Having had enough of my outlandish behavior and drunken spells, my father suggested the kids and I pack up and move to my brother Chad and his girlfriend Tori's house in California. "We can help you," they claimed. "You can stay with us for as long as you need." I was not getting any better where I was, and I was only adding destruction and demise to my endless track record. Dad didn't know what to do with me anymore. He was done—done with finding empty Crown bottles because I had ran out of beer; finished with the lies; done with the heartache. No parent wants to watch a child self-destruct before their very eyes. So that's where Chad came in. An opportunity—a way out—appeared to be knocking at my door. So I agreed to take Jayden and Annie and move to California. I didn't have a lot of options at that point. My breaking point had occurred. I could no longer adequately care for my own children.

The idea was that getting me out of my present surroundings would help me dry out. Perhaps I could start a new life. The departure was my last vestige of hope for a way out of the dark well into which I had plummeted. I was not only dragging myself down but my children, too; and they certainly didn't deserve that. I was very sick and needed a miracle to pull me through. I often cried out for help, but the cry was not yet loud enough. I would have to lose it all. The trip to California would actually be the wrong turn that became the catalyst in setting me straight again.

It didn't really occur to me to worry about Bill taking the kids. The weekend before we left for California, he hadn't even come to pick up Jayden. And he yet to take Annie for a weekend. Was he infatuated with his girlfriend at the time and we were the least of his concern, or was he angry with me and this was his revenge? Whatever the reasoning, I know he knew it was wrong. It was time for his wake-up call as well. Deep down, I knew it was wrong to leave without warning, but I didn't think it would matter. So we did it anyway. I had to make a move. I would lose Jayden and Annie if I didn't get some help.

I didn't get out of town without an unexpected visit. The Department of Human Services (DHS) was searching for us in Tonkawa. Unaware of the circumstances but well informed of my drinking, they found us at a most unfortunate time. I pled with the compassionate social worker and explained that we were now homeless. I explained to her my plans to get help from my brother in California. He and his girlfriend were already on their way. And she sympathized. She agreed the best thing would be to get help, and fast. But it would still be too late. Proof was already in the books of my present state—I was a raging alcoholic, and I neglected my children. Not that I abused my children, but oftentimes I put them behind my number-one priority at that time: drinking. I didn't think I had a habit. I was oblivious to the fact that I was an alcoholic. The saying in AA rings true—when you start drinking again, it's the same as where you left off. But worse.

So, in August of 2009, Chad and Tori arrived to the rescue in their compact, maroon, two-door Mustang. We crammed the car with every belonging we could. Between Jayden, Annie, and I—and all the overstuffed suitcases, pink-dotted diaper bag, my long-forgotten Bible, laptop computer, toys, and tons of miscellaneous items—the car was packed to the brim. This was it, I thought. A start to our new life—a sober one, I hoped. But I wasn't done yet. Even before we left, I tried to sneak off to the Conoco store one last time for a sixer. The cheap beer would do. I got my way—I managed to scrape up enough change for a couple of natural light beers then hid the cans. I often resorted to natty light when I was low on cash...which was a lot of the time. I had plenty of my prescription Xanax to help take the edge off, though, and Chad and Tori had extras for backup. These pills were acceptable as far as they knew. They took them too! And hey, they were prescribed by a doctor. There was certainly enough to take the edge off, so surely I wouldn't completely freak out. Little did I know—or the doctor who gave them to me—that these tiny, blue oval pills would help pick up the pace to my insanity mode.

This is where our collective lack of knowledge was hurtful. My family—those that knew—had no clue as to just how dangerous those pills were. They were marked with a doctor's stamp, so that made them okay. The doc had first started me off with the low-dosage pink Xanax, but I had now progressed to the higher-dosage blue ones. Later, a different doctor would prescribe me blue Klonopin. The prescribing doctors were not aware that I was chugging the pills down with alcohol day after day, and I wasn't going to offer them this bit of information. These fine pills were powerful enough on their own—they didn't need the mixture of alcohol to deepen the effects twice more. But I didn't know that.

As we headed west, I received a phone call from a police officer telling us to turn the car around. But at my father's insistence, we kept on pressing forward. Dad was then visited by a policeman and Bill back in Tonkawa.

The kids and I reached California scot-free, and I began my first attempt at sobriety. I continued using my Xanax, which I would discover was not a safe call. Little did I know, my abstinence from alcohol would be short-lived. The kids' father was seeking us out—the same guy who had previously skipped out on picking the kids up for their weekend visit. But he had changed his mind, and it was probably for the best.

When the kids and I first arrived in Sacramento, I thought we were on the right track. And we might have progressed nicely, but fate had something else in mind. Jayden started karate class in the fall, and Annie started walking at nine months. I started back to school at the University of Phoenix online. We attended Trinity Life Church twice a week. I even made a public profession to the Lord for the second time, and Annie and Jayden were dedicated to Christ in front of the congregation. We all enjoyed fun-filled days in the park as we basked in the California sun. Small glimpses of hope shimmered all around us. Various bands at Willow Park played euphoric music, and Jayden and Annie and I clapped our hands to the beat of a new drum. They laughed and played, enjoying our outdoor activities, taking it all in. Annie swayed back and forth to the rhythm, looking at Mommy to follow suit, giggling ever so slightly. They were enjoying just being kids and enjoying their mom being free of alcohol. But those sweet days were soon shattered by the wreckage of the storm. Oh, how I longed for that sweet, summer music once again. Perhaps someday,

Jayden and Annie in California, 2009

in another context when life changed for the better and destiny took its course, it would return. Or maybe the music would be different next time. A different kind of sweetness.

Back then, I was deceived by my own blindness. Obviously, there was more to learn, more to discover. The beautiful gift of sobriety had not yet embraced me in its healing powers. I wasn't ready. I grudgingly found my way to more bottomless pits before I learned to appreciate life and the gifts waiting at my doorstep. The dreadful disease tore at me once again, ripping apart any beauty still intact. Dreadful demons ate me alive with every chug of a Bud Light bottle, every pop of a pill. I gave into these monsters, swallowing pink- and blue-colored pills, washing them down with twelve-packs of Bud Light at a time. I couldn't resist. Sometimes I would melt the pill in my mouth so it would hit me harder; drown the pain faster. My body became enslaved by these bitter-tasting pills. What was worse, I still craved more. Those cravings polluted my body and flushed out my brain, steadily destroying God's masterpiece. Who I was did not matter anymore because I couldn't come to terms with her. Defeated and drained, I sadly took for granted the most important gifts in my life thus far: Jayden and Annie

Three months after the kids and I moved to California, Dad informed me that he'd received a letter stating that a judge had granted temporary custody of the children to their father Bill, and Jayden and Annie must be brought back to Oklahoma. There was very little time to build any defense. Attempts at trying to find an attorney with such short notice miserably failed. Destiny had a different plan. This was unfortunate, but I had it coming. I could not escape from this treacherous disease and the reality of what I had become forever. I could no longer escape my long trail of sin. The fast lane I'd traveled in for so long had come to a dead end, with no way around. Life quickly came to a screeching halt, and I was blinded by the dust. It would be a while before the dust cleared. I did not consciously choose to begin taking this road, but once there, I couldn't seem to find an exit.

Had I really reached this point of no return? Perhaps there was one more deck of cards to be dealt, one last chance. Perhaps my new hand of cards would be a better deal. I would settle for fair at this point. Or was this one of the those hazy dreams where I would wake up to find the sun streaming through the window, reminding me that breakfast had to be made and backpacks and diaper bags had to be filled and zipped before that one last dash out the door to make it to Sunrise Elementary School, just up the road on Tyler Street. On the surface, I appeared no different from any other mother taking her child to school on a busy day. Holding Jayden's hand, approaching the preschool, Annie wrapped tightly around my hip—I was living that dream for a moment. And then I woke up.

CHAPTER 4

The Beginning
of the End

When I was eleven years old, I pretended to be a mother, even though I was not yet interested in boys. In my fantasy, I was the rightful owner of two beautiful children. I would take the little girl to dance in her pink leotard and ballerina shoes, the boy to baseball practice in his all-star ball cap and matching uniform. I strongly desired a family of my own someday, despite the fact that my own was torn apart. Maybe it was a strange fixation at this stage of my life—desiring such a grown-up thing. Nonetheless, they were innocent thoughts, unscathed by the world outside. But then the fantasies stopped. Somewhere along the way, my fixation shifted and I became heavily influenced by my surroundings. I began to want what the world wanted. Finally, temptations got the best of me, and I gave into my surroundings. These temptations would soon take over who I was—the person God had created me to be. By the time I actually conceived those children I'd so dearly imagined, I was unable to appreciate the blessing because addiction consumed my life. To get back to the place God wanted me to be, I would have to lose everything to realize my true potential in life.

T*hump, thump, thump.* Persistent knocking at the door startled me. The Batman shirt I'd picked out for Jayden to wear to preschool that day dropped to the floor. It was seven o'clock in the morning, another school day. But the early morning knock at the door stopped us all in our tracks. "Who is it, Mommy?" Jayden was curious. But I was speechless, and fear shot through my five-foot-seven frame like a speed rocket. I knew what this concerned before I tightly and reluctantly gripped the doorknob. I wished I didn't have to open that door. But, ready or not, it was time to face the future. At the time, the future did not appear hopeful.

The thought of ever being separated from my children was inconceivable. Jayden's appearance was that of a true California kid with his soft blond hair and deep blue eyes. But his persona was quite the opposite. He was a sweet and funny five-year-old with Oklahoma roots to match. Annie was more independent; her green eyes and baby-fine brown hair suited a smart little baby, pretty and delicate, wise beyond her ten months of life. But they were both sweet beyond belief, naturally deserving of their mommy's love for them, which wasn't always communicated when she drank. Yet they were forgiving. And thank God, despite all that would happen, they are normal, happy kids.

That morning as I got Jayden ready for school—favorite Batman shirt, matching shorts, and black Nike shoes—I knew something was different, and fear bubbled under the surface. That deep ingrained fear never quite seemed to go away. It lingered in my life, searching for something to attach itself to. Like a bat in a cave, it went away in the presence of light but thrived in the darkness. Certainly my life had become accustomed to the darkness. It's like you know something is about to go down before it occurs, but you just can't place your shaky finger on it. That aching in your stomach—it's not from lack of food but instead from lack of something immeasurable. I think it's meant to be that way, because if you knew ahead of time the tragic events to come, you might just do something stupid. This could be God's little way of preparing us, of warning our spirits before we are consciously aware. If only I would have listened to those cautions the first time.

But this morning, I opened the door, and there she boldly stood—my worst nightmare come true, blatantly staring back at me. A uniformed woman officer was there to take my children. My time was up. It was too late to be saved now; this was no longer in my hands. It was obviously in Bill's.

A social worker from child services was with the policewoman. She asked specific questions regarding Annie. I could tell she'd done this type of call hundreds of times. Whether this take-away was justified or not didn't matter—it was just her job. And my actions left enough reasoning for it to be justified.

The social worker asked if I had more formula. She wanted me to fetch her a bag with clothes and diapers. Why? Where were they going? This was all happening way too fast. Outside, a gentleman was talking on the phone. Dressed in suit and tie, he was ready for action. "We got them." I heard him report into his phone. I suspect Bill was on the other end. The deal was done, and they had won. My sins of the past would not be forgiven and were to be heavily judged. I had a lot to prove. Bill strongly resented me. I was not worthy of forgiveness but was now subject to judgment and ridicule. I had it coming to me, and I would have to pay. The spotlight was now off of him and onto me because the devil had something here. But who could blame them for judging me? The social workers didn't know me; they were just acting on what they'd been told. And the attorney was getting his money. But however you put it, I was the bad guy.

At that moment, I felt completely and utterly helpless. But perhaps to be helpless is exactly what I needed. I had no power to stop this. I had lost my precious angels, my gifts from God—all because of bad choices brought on by a destructive disease I no longer wanted any part of. It was not fun anymore, and the fun was never worth it. I hadn't asked for this, yet it sought me out and had me at hello. It now had all of me and it was relentless, ripping me apart and my family, too. It tore at my worn flesh, leaving open wounds in desperate need of healing. The wounds needed opportunity to heal, but there had to be an open door. I could not do this alone.

Scrambling for papers, I hoped for a miracle. An official document, any excusable evidence to prevent the take-away.

But my search left me empty-handed and with no rescue in sight, I broke down. I tried desperately to hold it together, but I sank to the floor and began to sob frantically. The kids did not need to see their mom in any more disarray than they already had—I knew that. The woman officer seemed to feel my pain. "I'm afraid it's time for us to go now," she said, sounding like she felt sorry for me. But no one was there to save us from what was about to occur. Slowly, reluctantly, I got up. For a moment, time stood still. I took Jayden back to the bedroom, explaining that everything would be okay and not to worry. I desperately wanted us to all be okay. I hadn't touched a drink in over ninety days, but this didn't mean anything to them. I had messed up too many times. I no longer could be trusted.

The social worker peered into the bedroom where I was holding the kids in my embrace just one last time. "I'm sorry, miss, but it's time for us to go now," she repeated. She took Jayden's hand away from my own and placed Annie in her car seat. She loaded them into the car, and I followed to say goodbye. Looking at Jayden's distraught face, I was at a loss for the right words to say. I was now powerless. I had reached yet another dead end. The kids trusted me, and I had let them down. I had lost control of not only my life but my children's lives, as well. I desperately needed rehab; there was no leveraging here.

And this is the way it should have been. There were kids involved. I looked at my two innocent children in the backseat—Jayden confused and my sweet baby girl so oblivious, happily playing in her car seat, as a normal, happy baby would. Neither were aware they would not be waking up alongside Mom anymore, at least not for a while. I shut the car door. There was nothing I could do. The now emotionless social worker started the engine. And like that, they were gone.

I was now branded—by myself as well as those around me—as an incompetent mother, an alcoholic, a failure. From now on, cold eyes would observe me; they would fail to look past the wrong and refuse to see the new all because I was bombarded with illness and captivated by darkness.

Through all the despair, and the diseased mind, body, and soul, there was someone willing to see the beauty that was meant to be—I just didn't know Him anymore, and therefore, I couldn't see what He could see. I had to find Him again.

CHAPTER 5

A False Start

Another one of those daydreams, this time as a teen. I fantasized about going to California to become an actress or model. I pursued this dream. I contacted agencies not only in California, but all over the world. I was never tall enough, but I continued trying anyway. Unfortunately, that dream amounted to one modeling ad and almost an appearance on The Love Boat. *Funny. I was underage, so I needed a parent signature. Grandma had told me to tell them I was eighteen, but I just couldn't do it. I pursued my dream hard and begged to be allowed to go to Casablanca Modeling School. I convinced Dad to take me to a movie audition once. The point at which I gave up on this dream is the point where my focus began to change again. I became pregnant with Jayden, so I aimed at college. I was a single mother and wanted a better life for us. However, I had been pursuing a broadcast and journalism degree, which didn't seem realistic with a child. When I went back, I returned as a business major because of its versatility. So I did finally make it to California—on a foundation of broken dreams. Who would have imagined, looking into that crystal ball, that I would move to California, only to become a dry drunk?*

Since moving to the Golden State and attempting sobriety, I had managed to refrain from alcohol. Hey—I had my prescription pills to help me with the edge and tide me over. After all, they were "prescription." But in reality, the doctor's remedy only deepened my depression. And if I dared to go without it, fear would catapult my mind and body into a tailspin. Nonetheless, we were all proud of my abstinence from alcohol. When, astonishingly, I hit the three-month mark, Tori presented me with my ninety-day AA chip, which read, "To thine own self be true." At the time, this phrase held no significance for me whatsoever. Maybe if I had actually learned what this meant and where it came from, I would have strived to make it a constant reality. But you can't yearn for something you know nothing about.

I only thought I knew what sobriety was back in those gloomy, lifeless days. I thought I needed all those meds for my wandering mind and my frazzled nerves. I was mistaken. My doctor prescribed dosage upon dosage of Xanax, clearly believing my problems could be bandaged with a .5 milligram pill. Now the doctor added Klonopin to the mix. I would later learn these pills were not only horribly addicting, but they actually fed my anxiety, twice more. At this point, the damage was already done. My list of dependences was now further extended and so were my problems! No sooner did I refill my prescriptions, then it was time for another doctor's visit. My monthly fill no longer satisfied me. Time and time again, the doctors and nurses accepted my plea. They never let me down.

Waking up alone at Chad and Tori's was a harsh reality I didn't want to get used to. Once my kids were gone, I cried myself to sleep every night; my pillow would be sopping wet from the tears that fell from my swollen eyes. My kids were my only real motivation for fighting this disease, and now they were gone. This time when I lost the fight, the blow sent me crashing down. I had no more fight in me—at least not from the view on the hard, cold floor.

I had my little blue pills, but it wasn't long before the bottle was empty. I then needed another fix; something that would enable me to forget, again and again. I desired an endless dose. At this point, approaching the dead end I had so frequently visited was an easy trip. I had no tools to work with; nothing to prevent me from the next drama waiting to unfold. If I had tried to get sober the right way, I would have reached into my work belt and grabbed the largest hammer to beat away temptation. I would have found my rock to stand on. However, I did not know what the right way was, and I certainly had no tools, much less a work belt to put them in. So, like a champ, I hopped in my brother's Jeep Cherokee and drove straight to the Hillstone liquor store. The drive was short, a mere two blocks away, and I made darn sure I had my larger purse. That way I could stash away more bottles. I was reluctant to buy the alcohol at first, but it didn't take long until I seeped of poison from head to toe.

Later I realized this was the point where I truly lost control…if that was possible in my morbid state. The friends of AA always say that if you go back to your addiction, you start right back where you left off, and it usually gets worse. This was not good for me because I was last found at the bottom of the barrel. When you hit the bottom of the drum, death is not far behind.

My first trip to the store was excusable in Tori's eyes, because of the tragic events that had just taken place. Heck, Tori even drank one with me. "Now, don't be going back for more," Tori remarked. Chad remained silent. He knew me all too well. But surely, it would be okay for just this time. I was lying to myself, which was nothing out of the ordinary. I was doomed at the first whiff of it. Just the smell of it drew my lips to its short neck like a love affair gone wrong. On my second trip to the store, I bought the mini bottles so I could easily stash more in my purse.

My false sense of reality said I was ready for more game. But I had already lost before I even hit the play button. I went back time and time again for those mini bottles. Farther and farther away from reality I once again flew. Alcohol gave me a false sense of pride and security that got me into trouble every time. So what happened next was not surprising.

When sober, I am not ever the type to speak what I think at first glance. Some women are quick to speak their minds; well, that's not me. And when I try to be something I'm not, I look like a clown. I usually keep my thoughts to myself—especially at times when I needed to speak out the most. This is who I was. But the alcohol reversed this tendency in me. That false sense of security kicked in, and I discovered that I now had an increased confidence to speak up. Having just lost my kids to CPS (in California DHS was called CPS), I had much to speak about, although no one really wanted to hear it, and it was certainly told in the wrong context. The insanity had begun.

"Have you been drinking again?" Tori and Chad hit it right on the head.

"Yes, I'm drinking. What are you going to do about it?"

"Huh?"

"I'm not scared of you!" The insanity continued until one swing at the head sent me tumbling to the cold, hard tile. Tori didn't mess around. I had a big, black eye to prove it. Her six-foot frame against my stumbling self left me little chance for defense. Not surprisingly, I got the boot; this time I carried a reminder on my swollen face. Tori and Chad—like everyone else—were done helping me. And how could they— they needed help themselves. Lonely, afraid, and battered and bruised, I was once again at the bottom of the drunk tank. It was a short trip this time.

I managed to find my way to a friend's apartment a few places down. Stumbling, I climbed up the stairs and crashed at her front door. But this door remained shut in my face as well. Next, I looked up to find two husky police officers ready to take me in. But they weren't taking me to the jailhouse. Instead they took me to the Holiday Inn, conveniently next to the airport. They didn't want to deal with me either. This was my quiet invitation to leave California and go back to Oklahoma. The Golden State was not so appealing anymore.

The police officers may have dropped me off at the Holiday Inn, but this was no vacation. Cashless, I asked the concerned receptionist if I could borrow the phone for a collect call. My shaky finger began dialing the only number I ever remembered. Dad picked up on the other end and, thankfully, accepted the call. In moments, I was scheduled for takeoff. Flight 571 for Oklahoma City was scheduled for the next day at the break of dawn. I sat there in the empty hotel room with my body so craving the alcohol that would relieve its strain. Not surprisingly, I found it fit to take a little excursion down to the nearest convenience store—six blocks away. The Conoco store would not sell me a six-pack of bud light; they said I was already drunk. Well, I was not! However, that didn't slow me down. I was on a mission. I walked another five blocks to another Conoco. Bingo! Needless to say, it was a long walk back.

By the time I reached my seat on the airplane, I once again needed to quench my thirst. More mini bottles at my disposal—this time, in the luxury of a 747 jetliner. And to that I added my Klonopin, and I was flying high. Stopping in Denver along the way, I helped myself to the airport bar where I met a new friend. She must have been crazy just like me. Oh, to imagine the sight of me. Black eye, stumbling about, talking nonsense. "Yeah, my brother's girlfriend knocked me out, kicked me out, and now look at me!" The trip back was smooth sailing—I just remained drunk the whole time. And before I knew it, touchdown. Welcome to Oklahoma, home sweet home. And, just like that, my new start in California was history.

CHAPTER 6

A Vicious Cycle

The saying goes, once you've lived in Oklahoma and move away, you always find yourself longing to go back. You know...that southern drawl, the comfort of close-knit families, and backyard barbecues.... You want to get back to that well-known Oklahoman sense of comfort and belonging.

But as I returned to Oklahoma without my children, I didn't feel like I belonged. Even in the security of my own people, I was secluded. This was the place where I had gotten sick and hit a bottom I couldn't get out of. It was the place for old people, places, and things. But the problem was not my home, it was me. I was my own worst enemy, unable to escape from the demons within. I did not yet know that the cure to my disease was waiting around the corner. I just didn't know where to look for it.

My first shot at sobriety was short-lived. Just another failure in my life thus far. I should have known it wouldn't be smooth sailing. The turbulent waters were more than this boat could handle. I required more strength. I had thought California was the open door I needed to start over, but it quickly shut in my face. It would have been convenient to first peek inside, but life doesn't work that way. Life for me revolved around one mess after another—an endless merry-go-round. True recovery would take time. After all, I didn't wind up in an alcoholic stupor overnight; surely I couldn't expect to ditch the habit overnight. I might have been born again, but this meant I now had work to do. God was working, but I had to trust Him. A large order for my altered mind. It was time to eliminate all mind-altering substances. My wretched addiction to anxiety pills still remained, and the fierce anxiety continued to control my mind, pulsating through my thoughts. I could not be the woman God designed me to be until I eliminated the bad girl and sent the lost girl—the one so easily persuaded by the world—back to the pit she came from.

By the time I got to the airport in Oklahoma City, I was as high as a kite. But in reality, my kite hadn't even made it off the ground. Brokenhearted and hopeless, I was unsure of the next step. An old party friend picked me up at Will Rogers World Airport. Kassie was much younger than me; she was nineteen years old. Nonetheless, she appeared mature beyond her years. She was highly social and friendly, all with a cute little figure to boot. But this girl knew nothing about what I actually needed. I'd been talking to her on Facebook while in California, and I now explained to her my dilemma. "You can come and stay at my house," she assuredly proclaimed. Great, another point of rescue. Nonetheless, I was once again out of options, and I was desperate. Not many people were willing to take me in at this point. After all, she had a nice apartment and was honorably discharged from the army due to injury. Surely she had her act together. Nightfall quickly fell upon us as we drove back to Ponca City, my new temporary home and the place my kids, now with their father, called home. The darkness revealed the pain lingering inside me waiting to ignite once again. My body was bloated and pale on the outside, and darkened and deprived on the inside. I needed a fix of something quick so as to continue to blanket the pain and feed the devil.

It was December, but I wasn't feeling the holiday spirit. I arrived in Ponca City at Kassie's apartment wearing my long, black coat—the perfect disguise. In it, I felt I could hide myself from the shame and guilt. I also hid beneath a red and gray OU hat. I slapped the hat on my head to help hide my blank, dreary eyes. Eyes once again fearful of the unexpected. Arriving back home was both frightening and tantalizing, to say the least. Temptation had already met me at the door.

Kassie's apartment found me coming and going. I would drink the place dry, then have to vacate. I waited until Dad was on the road trucking and then made an excuse to visit his home, where I always managed to find a taker. That is, someone to fetch me alcohol so I could be numb again. I was never violent. But I was hopeless, physically and mentally distraught. Kassie was my new partner in crime and knew of drug connections to hook us up, if need be. What I really needed was to be hung out to dry. But instead of drying out, things got worse again. In my destructive quest of nonsense, I added cocaine to the mixture. Now it was pills, booze, and street drugs—the right mixture for spiraling me deeper down the hole. Luckily, I could still breathe. But often times it was difficult. Oddly enough, the hardest time to catch my breath was not when I was suffering from the toxins but when I was held captive by my own wandering mind. I remained in a tough battle between heaven and hell. Although my earthly body and soul no longer cared, the heavenly seed implanted in me since birth awaited the opportunity to germinate. It needed encouragement; a glimpse of hope. After all, hope is what we all need.

Even in the midst of all the heavy drug and alcohol abuse, I continued crying out for help. In the seclusion of Kassie's small bathroom, frantically sobbing and down on my knees, I called my preacher from Trinity Life Church back in Sacramento. Desperation filled my creaky voice. I so desired a way out. For good. I imagined a preacher would suffice. I had acquired the willingness, but could I follow through? Getting help was what I wanted, but I had no clue of who could possibly help me this time. But it wasn't meant for me to wonder, but rather to trust. There was no magic wand, that's for certain. A hit over the head with a beer bottle knocking some sense into me? But I might rebel. Over and over, I looked for excuses to continue in my morbid state. Extreme caution was to be used for my emotionally needy state. Only God knew what would get through to me, and assuredly He would make sure I received it. Getting humble was on the list. The list had other items, too.... But not just for me—for others, too. His plan was for me to reach out to others. With the new me. With this book.

This was one of life's callings. Not to be an alcoholic—that was a given—no, He intended me to be an overcomer. Although I had made some wrong choices in my life—some very bad ones at times—I was still God's child. We all are.

During this time, I was allowed supervised visitation with Jayden and Annie. I was lucky to get to see them at all, but that didn't make it any easier. We met twice at the Ponca City McDonald's, in the same town I so heavily partied in. Both times the visits resembled a far-out dream. A dream gone wrong by all accounts! It wasn't really me. We were supposed to be at home together, just the three of us reading stories and playing make-believe. Well, this was certainly no make-believe. It was reality. I had allowed all this to happen. I regretted not reaching out sooner. It was now too late. In this game called drug abuse, the victims cannot afford to wait. Addiction is like a vulture, sucking the target dry of life. The victims scream out earnestly, if they make it that far, but few hear their cry because it blends in with the world.

I had failed as a mother; I was no longer trusted with my own children. I was a mom whose future with her children would now be controlled by some stranger unaware of my true identity—a person that God wanted to use for His very own kingdom. The judge could not have the final say forever. For now on the outside I appeared desolate, dark, and hopeless. For now, Jayden and Annie were motherless. But this too, was only temporary.

The kids arrived at McDonald's with Bill and his niece. She walked with him in his new life as a full-time dad. God's hand had revealed itself again through his life. A few short months before, Bill would have never taken the kids, but my sickness forced him to think otherwise. It seemed now he had gotten his priorities straight.

Annie and me at McDonalds in Ponca City, 2009.

Finally, after weeks of not seeing my children, they were here. They looked even more beautiful than before. This was the encouragement I needed to step on it. It was time to punch into high gear and ride this thing out to the end. Nothing could stop me now. Except for the twelve-pack I would be buying at the end of our visit. You know, to take the pain down a notch. But still, I had a deeper urge to plow this disease deep down to the depths of the earth where it came from. But it was hard to see through the thick glaze that fogged my view. I required assistance to move ahead to where I belonged—rehab. Amid the foggy view, a sweet glimmer of hope had now wrapped itself around me.

Annie appeared much thinner. Jayden was happy to see me but leery. His blue eyes stared intently, curiously, at his mommy who had once always been there for him but no so much anymore. What was Mom up to now? I was to blame for their confusion. More than ever before, I desperately wished that I had never taken that first wine cooler.

A custody court date had been scheduled since arriving back in Oklahoma, and with it fast approaching, it was time to have a game plan. I could no longer escape the demons of my past and present. I was ready for a fight, although I needed much training in the ring. Did I, or anyone for that matter, expect me to offer anything of value about myself to the judge? A quick fix such as a thirty-day rehab would provide only a false sense of security. I needed to be taught how to live life again. To dance and sing, to shout to the rooftops the news of my new freedom. There had to be a way for me to reach to the heavens and remain in that beauty forever. But how would I get there? And who would help me?

Mr. Bilford, my dad's attorney, came to Kassie's house with the layout. The first step for progression was to attend AA meetings. Kassie offered to go along for the ride. But the thought of admitting defeat made my pulse race. Suddenly, I needed a drink so I could swallow. Gulp. "Oh yes," I said, "I'll go." But once again, the ravaging bottle stole my plans. The moment I stepped out of the house, I thirsted for more. "Can we go to the convenience store?"

Hard discipline would have done me some good at this point. The constant bleeding on the inside would not stop. And so, I became numb. Numb to the world and my own family; to my own children, I was miserably numb. It's clear the devil uses addiction to destroy lives and capture souls. It's just one of his many schemes, and I happened to be a victim of this one. Sadly, there are many more victims who are never accounted for. Nonetheless, that lost seed still planted within me was anticipating fresh water.

CHAPTER 7

Van's House

I got a DUI when I was twenty-one years old—which is not unusual for this day and age. It seemed all my friends had at least one. My DUI classes were next to a two-story house. Men came and went out of this mystery house. I watched from a distance, unaware I would soon be coming and going from my own mystery house. I was told these men lived in a sober house. They got in trouble, had addictions, and so forth. I never thought twice about them. Perhaps I should have. I went to my one-hour class on drugs and alcohol, then after class, I popped a cold one. After all, that's what people my age did. Twentysomethings did not go to sober houses. I didn't even know what that was before now. Boy, was I in for a rude awakening. If I had only known what I know now. The path I chose would lead me straight to a place like that, but God has allowed me

to see the rough edges along the way so that I could appreciate
His glory.

The idea of rehab had never sounded so good. This was the ray of hope my heart now desired. But it was not instant gratification. If I had known I was the ideal candidate for this years ago, perhaps the ride might have been smoother. Now the ride lagged behind, waiting to throw me off. I feared the unknown, but my life was not my own, anyhow. I needed coaxing and discipline, and I needed it fast. God knew this. That's why it was the right timing. I required a miracle in my present state of mind. Even physically, I was distraught. No longer model material, I was now bloated with alcohol, my hands swollen, my dark, distant eyes no longer approachable. I needed to be rescued before my worn body came to rest beneath a blackened tombstone. Help was on the way—it was, in fact, just fifty-seven miles to the southwest. With Dad's help, I was on my way to a sober house named Van's House in Enid, Oklahoma.

A week before we left for Van's House, as part of the intake process, I had undergone an analysis of my ravaging addiction. I was well prepared for my official title of "addict," documented and all. We all knew I was sick, but my problem required an accurate diagnosis. My prognosis was deep. The analysis indicated the extent of my disease. It was a detailed—graphic, if you will—description of my greatest weakness. The best of the best, no less. Documentation is so prevalent in cases like mine, often making its way into courts as justification for wrongdoing. The paperwork could certainly be used against me, but this was just part of the process. Once officially branded an alcoholic, the title could harm me for life. But this was the world's opinion of me. These critics were not the ones whose opinion mattered most. God knows no brands. Only His people. And I was one of those people. His creation. The thing about brands is, some brands fade and are made new by a bigger, better brand. It just takes time for people to adapt to the new brand. And some never adapt. Me? I was ready for a newer version.

As we pulled up in front of Van's House, my anxiety deepened. My palms began to sweat, and once again, I could not swallow. Seven-oh-one West Maine Street. An address I would soon be repeating every day at the end of AA meetings—"Here at 701 West Maine Street, we have a chip system honoring different stages of sobriety."

At first, my anxiety remained in overdrive. It would take some adjusting to line me out. But, although I didn't know it yet, I was safer now than I had ever been. This place would be my safety net for a year.

"Alisa, you know I love you, but I don't know what else to do," Dad sadly exclaimed. He knew I was scared. He was, too. Although he was sick of my actions, I was still his bright-eyed little girl. The girl who had always desired to make her daddy proud. At this point in life, most dads are walking their little girl down the aisle, not up to rehab. I was a disgrace to myself and others. If I had only understood the magnitude of God's unfailing love, this trip would have been nonexistent. But here I was. I had made it at last to Enid, Oklahoma. My new, profound hope. It was a long time coming, but it was the right time. There was no turning back now; at least not without a fight.

"When you're done here, you can start again. I'll help you." Dad was persistent. After all I had done, he still soothed me and held me close when I needed someone the most. He was a godsend and the best dad ever.

I reached for the doorknob—part of me reluctant, the other part simmering with hope. I could not see the road ahead. I only saw what I was at that moment. How I felt. What I longed for. I was right where I needed to be, in the moment. One day at a time.

As Dad and I entered the large, stone, two-story former funeral home, I found myself gasping for air. The anxiety was ever-present, and now it was pulsating in sync with my rapidly beating heart, making it hard to breathe. I went straight into a short meeting with Mr. Scott Van Krevelen; it was an intimidating one-on-one to say the least. Scott, a six-foot-two, husky, broad-shouldered, former OU football player—and a recovering alcoholic—captivated my attention. At least what was left of it. A copy of the serenity prayer hung on his wall, along with OU memorabilia and past and present achievements. I was unsure what to think of this man. He came off stern and firm. He didn't seem like someone who'd be fooled by me. And that was exactly what I needed. But there was something else, too. Maybe a tender heart, a loving soul. Something had to make him want to help the lost children of the world. After all, he had been one of them.

Scott's wife, Sally, was less intimidating. She was much shorter than Scott, with an athletic build. A magnificent woman on the inside and fanciful on the outside. She was the mothering type, but she was not as soft as she appeared. She couldn't be. She was tough and relentless; she would stop at nothing to make sure she gave these girls her best. The recovering addicts placed under her wing needed guidance from someone who could whip us rock-hard addicts into shape. And trust me, we needed a lot of shaping. Indeed, we needed mothering, but what we needed more was discipline and structure. Something the disease of addiction had taken away. We could benefit from someone we could relate with because the world had deemed us outcasts. Miss Sally was just the right cure for our ailment. Like Scott, she too was a recovering addict with thirty-one years of sobriety under her fanciful belt.

A house full of addicted girls was a scary conception. A load of girlfriends had never been my cup of tea. Truthfully, I preferred men over woman. Funny, other girls in the house claimed the same thing. Perhaps our personality types enabled our disease. Or, maybe we were all just really in the same boat. A boat rocked by the wavering winds of addiction, not ever really knowing where it came from, not ever knowing its destination. But most of us were now aware that the boat had come to a tipping point and must stop. For me, that tipping point started at the first tip of a Bud Light. And, well, my boat had arrived and foundered long ago. Now it needed assistance in becoming upright and seaworthy again. Van's house would provide this—a solid structure for starting anew and rebuilding all that was destroyed in the storms.

As Dad and I met with Scott in his office, he cut to the chase. "We highly recommend a one-year commitment, because this brings the best results." But I couldn't quite sink this idea into my head. I thought rehab was thirty days. Reasoning was a hard catch for me now, anyway.

"One *year*?" I resentfully replied. But I couldn't back down on this one. Although my flesh was quivering, deep down inside a different sensation stirred, a longing for peace and love. I could not deny this. My higher power knew I was ready. I could now break free of the disease that for so long imprisoned me.

Miss Sally further advised us that I might want to go get a few necessities. I could have slept in my clothes for days, for all I cared. Nevertheless, we headed off to Walmart. As Dad and I walked about the busy store, my cluttered brain was preoccupied with fear. Fear of how my body would react to change. Distress of how people would react to me. The unknown had always been a part of my life and shouldn't have been so scary. A move in the right direction was uncomfortable at first. But God had this, and the time had come to shred the fear to pieces. God desired me to take the front seat in my poorly maintained life, but for now I was still riding in the back.

Necessities remained few for me. I didn't have the patience for shopping, and it became too confusing for my feeble mind. A box of Marlboros would do, a set of pale brown-colored sheets, and a bedspread. I did not care about pretty pink sheets with decorative flowers. I wasn't there to impress anybody; that was the least of my worries. My plans were to get out quickly so I could get back to Annie and Jayden. My food selection was kept to a bare minimum. Cooking was now a pastime, so

I opted for cheese, bologna, crackers, chips, and some dark chocolate donuts for breakfast. It was as if I were in a race, grabbing whatever caught my eye and putting it in our cart. The sweaty palms and sticky, dry mouth had begun. Walmart stimulated the fire to my already frazzled nerves.

And here I was at this life-changing moment in time. My cry for help was being answered: hope beckoned from a long, narrow hallway at Van's House. Only life was found in these thick, shielding walls. It was time to proceed forward.

Dad drove me back to the house. "Alisa, this is for the best. I love you, but I have to go now." He once again wished me well and was on his way.

Gulping a huge swig from my water bottle, I turned and began making my way down the hall to the meeting room. It seemed a long stretch as I contemplated a complete withdrawal from the addiction that had held me prisoner for so long. At the end of the hall, scrambled voices radiated from the meeting room as if they were calling me forward into the light. The new girl of the house had arrived in all her misery and shame. As I drew closer to these voices, I was scared, but I also knew that it was time to trust. As I turned to enter that roomful of chairs filled with people like me, I again found it hard to breathe. But fresh air was within reach.

And there I sat in this meeting called AA, with my long, black overcoat and my dirty, red OU ball cap that could certainly have used a washing or two. But cleanliness was not my top priority at that moment. I sat next to a red-haired girl named Kelsey. She wasted no time in greeting me, and in that instant became my refuge. I was so worried about speaking, but she assured me I didn't have to. She explained that for many of these AA-ers, talking through their problems helped them. I told her that today would probably not be my day to break the ice. So I sat there with my head down, never attempting to meet eyes with anyone but this angel that graced my presence. What a miserable sight I must have been. But there was nothing these people hadn't seen before. We were all different, yet very much the same. Perhaps I was a reminder to someone of what they had once been. A reminder of the despair they once housed.

The meeting ended at 12:50. Then came announcements, followed by the Lord's Prayer. Next, it was time to go to the girls' house. The boys resided on the second floor at this location, and the girls lived in a house on South Hayes Street, a few miles away. This was one of their stringent yet effective rules. Too often, addicts are led astray by codependence and unhealthy relationships. At this point, it was time to work on self. Selfishness is a big element of addiction, so it is advised in the Big Book of Alcoholics Anonymous to work on self to pull though. The Big Book contained the AA's Twelve Steps for recovery, and I would use this as a guide for the next twelve months. Pulling into the driveway with Miss Sally, I was instantly greeted by several girls. No one was jumping for joy, but they were willing to help carry in my bags.

"Well, hi there. My name is Christina. You must be Alisa," remarked the tall, fortyish blonde who gently grabbed my bag out of my hand and placed it in her own. Christina informed me she was from Kansas. Her time here would end in August; she'd be graduating with her one-year chip. She appeared strong as far as the eye could see. This trait would soon reveal itself when she was forced to play mommy when girls broke the rules.

The two other girls followed suit with the remainder of my belongings, including three sorry bags of groceries. Stunned by their eagerness to help, I proceeded to the screen door. As I stepped into the house at 1606 South Hayes, I was not yet aware of how this place would change my life forever. If I had known, I would have been here a lot sooner. However, things happen when they are supposed to according to His great plan. And according to that plan, I was right on time. Any sooner, and I would have not been ready. I'm a slow learner, but that's the way God made me.

For the first few weeks of my stay, my big sister at the house was Becka. When newcomers arrive at Van's House, they are assigned a big brother or big sister to help them adjust to their new surroundings. Becka was also the head of the house at the time. She was firm but good-natured. After making our introductions, Becka explained that she, too, had a family at home. A teenaged son and a husband eagerly awaited her return. She also had a nursing job at stake. If she did not complete this program, she could lose her nursing license. Unexpectedly but not surprisingly, a bump in the road would soon throw Becka's plan off course.

I settled into a large room shared with three other girls. I got the top bunk. My first night in the girls' house was hell, as expected. My body felt electrified, missing what it had relied heavily on day after day for months on end since Annie was born. The burning flames of my sin continued, and my body craved the poison that ignited the blaze. The first few days would prove the hardest. I did not sleep that night, nor would I for three days after. I remember getting a call from Jayden on the third day. He was excited to talk to me, and the call gave me a new strength and increased motivation. It reminded me of why I was there to begin with. I thought if I worked hard in my recovery, I could reclaim what I had lost. I clung to that hope for the rest of my stay. I did not receive any more phone calls.

As I detoxed, I continually prayed, over and over, in a heap of dripping sweat. I was forced to move to a different room; one with an open bottom bunk, for fear of me falling off the top. The new, smaller room had only one girl for the time being, which suited me just fine. I do not believe she felt the same, and I did not experience a peaceful sleep. I can recall lying in that bunk on a bright, sunny day. My head seemed detached from my body. And that's what it was. Just a body. Inside that worn body, I was crying out to God. I could hear the sound of jets overhead from Vance Air Force Base. This loud noise was a continual reminder that life persisted on the outside. My children were waiting for me. I had to get through this.

Not even a month after my arrival, Scott made an unexpected visit to the girls' house. I was not yet aware that so many girls failed to complete the full year of the program. Thanks to Scott, I was broken in quickly. Several of us girls were in the garage smoking Marlboros when Scott burst through the door. We jumped to our feet, scared to death. Assuredly, Becka must have whizzed her pants.

"Get your stuff, Becka! You're outta here!"

"But I didn't do it! I swear!" This was her claim. A familiar rant for so many girls. But she was speaking to dead air. Scott was long gone. There was simply no room for tolerance in this ferocious war of heaven and hell.

A few days before, there had been suspicion that Becka was popping pain pills again. As a result, she was forced to take a drug test. As she must have known, the test came back positive for drugs. Van's House had a no-tolerance rule. If you used drugs or alcohol, you were out.

The next day, I was alone in the house—which I felt was better. Better for me and them. I hated people seeing me in this condition. Insecurity had swallowed me whole. In reality, I needed people. I needed *these* people. I was in danger from the drugs and alcohol still lurking in my body. I could not go through with the noon AA meeting, and it was a requirement for those not working. Afraid social anxiety would kick in, I refused to go. I didn't care about consequences yet. I was still in panic mode, my body in shambles.

Bam! Suddenly, the front door slammed open. The noise radiated through the still house. Apparently I wasn't the only one who didn't go to a noon meeting. I buried my head in the pillow so to hide from the thumping footsteps making their way closer to my room.

"Alisa! Uh, are you okay? Why aren't you at the noon meeting?" I knew that sweet voice. It was the red-haired angel, home early from her job at the mall. She walked over to my bed and put her hand on mine, clutching it tightly

"Hey girl, you're going to make it through this. I know it's tough now, but it will get better. Trust me, I know. I've been through the same thing. If nothing else, be strong for your kids."

Those words echoed through my spirit, bringing a bit of comfort that I had not felt in a long time. I clung tightly to them. Words like that are what helped me to press forward. Iridescent words from God. But I had yet to go through my toughest point there on South Hayes Street.

After yet another restless night, it was time to get the day started. Routine was part of the structure at Van's House. The cycle was to put God into our everyday routine, along with chores and rules worth abiding by. We started each morning at six o'clock, with a chant of the serenity prayer followed by a reading of the twenty-four-hour book. Then a daily declaration of how we were going to stay sober.

"Just for today, I'm going to stay clean and sober. Just for today, I'm going to walk in God's will and not my own. Just for today, I'm going to…" And you fill in the blank. Most days, the blank would be filled in by something in the twenty-four-hour book. Ironically, this day for me, I would fill in the blank with "trust in God."

The afternoon slowly approached. Not working made the hours drag on. I made my way to the garage for a smoke. Not that it ever relieved any stress, but it was something to do to pass the time. It was also a time to talk with the other girls concerning daily occurrences of the house, like who was breaking the rules or who stole the bottle of perfume or who was drinking the bottle of Scope. But today at this moment, I was alone. Puffing away is the last thing I remember.

Next thing I knew, I was flat on my back on the concrete floor. Emily and Lara, the two girls at home at the time, came running to my rescue. The sight of me on the floor, passed out, mouth wide open, must have freaked them out. They didn't know what was going on with me; they only knew they had to call 911.

The ambulance arrived within minutes. Neighbors wondered what could possibly be going on now at the girls' house. It was not the first set of sirens at that house, and it would not be the last. Regaining consciousness, I opened my eyes to see a young, handsome EMT bending over me, asking me to recite my full name. But I could not respond to his urgent request. I couldn't remember my name! This scared me the most. Even with all the heavy drinking and drug abuse, I had never before experienced such a malfunction of the brain. Yet my addiction was the cause of the seizure. My body was so hugely unfamiliar with this new territory of cleanliness, it had gone straight into shock. The Xanax, in particular, was the most incriminating cause of the fall.

On the ride to the hospital, I began to regain my senses. I remembered my name, vaguely. Once at the hospital, the visit was surprisingly short. Scott and Sally arrived in a flash. Scott assumed perhaps I was using, but the doctor quickly eased his concern. The doctor wrote me a prescription to help me transition off the Xanax more smoothly. Quitting cold turkey with an addictive drug such as Xanax can cause seizures, and it is extremely dangerous. No one knew, including myself, exactly the extent of my addiction to these pills. I had been prescribed three .5 milligram Xanax per day, but sometimes I took more.

Needless to say, I was a lucky girl. God was clearly in sight. I just needed to further wipe the smudge from my eyes.

After my seizure, things got better. Bit by bit. One day at a time. The skies will pour rain before the sunlight breaks through so that its heavenly rays are more keenly felt. My life had approached the gateway to hell, I had felt the flames singe my clothing. I screamed loudly for help. Then suddenly, a jolt—and I was saved from that undesirable journey. That sudden jolt was God Himself, offering a sturdy rope to climb back to the top. The sturdy rope was Van's House, and I responded gratefully. My grasp was now firm and strong. In the face of death and darkness, this rope became my reassurance of a life worth living. I needed to be shown that light could overcome the darkness that encompassed me. I needed to be reminded that there could be sunlit days; that I could provide a beam of bright light to shine on my children. I was at the right place now for that.

After six weeks at Van's House, I saw Jayden and Annie again. Though still in rehab, it was a good start. It was time to haul off the wreckage, to make a better life for us all. Van's House would teach me to build this life from scratch. Through program and procedure but most of all, through God. Six weeks couldn't come soon enough and our time together was short-lived. Dad continued to bring the kids over for several more weeks. Van's House allowed weekend passes for residents who had gained approval from Scott and Sally. Finally, I was able to drive myself to pick up my kids. I did not have a place of my own, so we stayed at Dad's house. We spent our time wisely—reading, taking walks in the park, and just being with each other. Even the smallest increments of time spent together were much appreciated. At this point, I took nothing for granted and was learning the meaning of gratefulness. My kids were learning too. They were grateful to have their mom back!

God introduced me to the right people, and they served as guiding lights to help me in my recovery. I grew to love all of them very much. Both the AA program and Van's House required participants to obtain a sponsor. This sponsor would be an accountability partner, guiding us through the twelve steps of the program. I knew my sponsor the minute I saw her. She was very pretty, with sandy-colored shoulder length hair and a killer smile. She was calm, cool, and collected. We instantly connected. And so, I asked Jeanie to be my sponsor, and she graciously accepted. This connection allowed me to open up to someone, to share my faults, disappointments, and failures. She was there for me on my Fourth Step, at which point I had to take a moral inventory of myself and admit my wrongs to God and another human being. I am thankful I could confide in her.

So many special people like Jeanie existed at Van's House. And they became my refuge. Some found it hard to adjust to the light. But for me, I drew near and desired more of it. The day came when I got to be that light for somebody else, a new resident named Amy. Just two short months after representing death myself, I represented hope for someone else. When Amy first walked through the door, I met a familiar face of despair, my mind now clear enough to see it. It's like I was staring back at myself. In the end, Amy and I would be each other's strength. We, too, had a special connection written in

Christina, Amy, Kelsey, Emily, and me
at the girls' house, 2010

Annie, Jayden, and me,
Christmas 2010

stone. We both made it through the program successfully. But there were many who were not so lucky.

After seeing Christina graduate, my determination kicked into high gear. I too, wanted to graduate with my one-year chip. And finally, that day came. I made it through the program successfully; a completely new person. I spent the morning of January 27, 2011, in constant prayer. I prayed that I would represent myself well. That I would be a strong woman who hungered for God, who would no longer desire that empty house. The windows there had shattered, and the sharp-edged glass had severed through my skin, the blood had dripped its stain on others. But now this house had been made whole. I now resided in the house of the Lord, and nothing that entered into this house could ever destroy it. Not even the addiction that had ripped me away from my kids.

I reflected on what I would say that day, a process that had started weeks before the big day. My loved ones were proud of who I had become. Some were surprised that I had made it through the dry-out phase. So many hearts I had broken. But it was time to start my continued journey of healing. It was a miracle that I was still standing. I was a living witness of deliverance from alcohol and drugs. This was all they needed to see. It didn't matter what I said. Thank you would have been enough. But I wanted to share my journey. Just like I'm doing now. I wanted my graduation day—my new birthday—to be perfect. A rebirth had indeed occurred.

Life in my newfound sobriety was like nothing else. I now had a chance to live life normally, without the remnants of addiction weighing me down. Life is so much better than before. It's better because I learned to appreciate life, and at the same time I discovered my purpose of helping others. If I hadn't gone through the misery, I could not have come to this realization.

After my experience at Van's House, I began to see my breaking point in a new light. That point in my life where I was broken by the chains of alcohol and drugs, where what I cherished most, my children, were taken away—that point was where I made the turn for the better. Although the pieces were broken, shattered, God helped me put them back together. Piece by painful piece, the end result would be God's masterpiece because I was redeemed. Just as God intended me to be.

I had also met my future husband, Dusty, at Van's House. Just before my year there ended, Dusty found it fit to introduce himself to me. He found me at church one Sunday morning and asked me for my number. How convenient. It was as if we were high schoolers, passing notes in class. In a way we were starting all over with love. Just like we had to learn to live again, we had to learn about relationships and love again. And then, one weekend, there he was at the Ponca City Walgreens. We made eye contact, and life for us was never the same. He began attending my church in Ponca, as well. And this is where I met his adorable daughter Addi. You could tell she was crazy for her daddy. Likewise, he was one proud dad. This touched my heart, and I, too, wanted to be a part of loving this man. Another prayer came true, and God had much more in store for us.

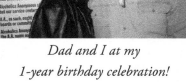

Dad and I at my
1-year birthday celebration!

My 1-year graduation at
Van's House, January 2011.

CHAPTER 8

The Big Day

Court was another dreadful event, but it was totally inescapable. I'm sure I'm not the first to admit that. I had never been to a court hearing regarding child custody before, and I was fearful. My first court appearance was because that DUI at the ripe old age of twenty-one had not happened on good terms. Judge Long's closing remark on my case was "I don't want to see you in these courtrooms again." He knew I didn't belong there. But this new court date wasn't a game to be played with. There were no guarantees. I needed a divine intervention.

I had high hopes that this court appearance would end in success. I hoped that my two babies would be coming home with their momma. After all, my life had changed for the better. I had beaten the odds and made it through a whole year of the program successfully. Glory to God—I was saved, and my children had their mother back, at lease in spirit. In actuality, I feared this day. Ironically, I had just achieved my one-year sobriety birthday a few days before court. The timing seemed perfect. I planned to take my seat on the stand and speak the truth about who I was then and who I had become, all the while admitting my wrongdoing. I was used to doing that now. The program had provided me with the tools I needed to face life's most daunting obstacles.

I wanted to put God on His throne even if I was the one on trial. I could practically taste sweet victory. Despite my wrongdoing, I was still Jayden and Annie's mother. I had loved them in my womb, and I loved them now. Nothing would change that. Not even some stupid disease. Not even the prosecutors. I was well aware that I had messed up; I didn't need reminding. But I hadn't always been bad. Sweet memories still remained, and I was hopeful this rang true for Jayden and Annie, too. I knew I was a winner in God's eyes and wished everyone else could see the same. But wishful thinking had no place in the courtroom.

It's often difficult for hurt loved ones to see through the debris of destruction. Not everyone can forgive like God does. And from the outside, it was difficult to see any good in a situation such as mine. Perhaps I still felt sheltered from Van's House, a supportive environment where I was forgiven and accepted despite my past. But it was still a cruel, hard world out here, and my seclusion from it could not last forever.

Reality quickly set in. Bill and his attorney were not concerned with what I had learned or how I had changed.

Neither was Judge Martin. Their concern was with my past, not my future—typical attitudes in cases like mine. I was the one who had messed up and gotten caught. My mistakes were on display for all to see. I had never quite thought I would be in the spotlight this way. But I believed that God would turn this addiction into one of my greatest blessings. I became infatuated with admitting my wrongs and pleading before the judge that I was a new person. I would promise to be a better mother. After all, God was a part of my life now. I had successfully completed the one-year program, I had graduated college with my bachelor's degree, and had gotten a new home. But this appeared insufficient in the wake of my past. Too many others had failed before me. I was paying not only for my own mistakes, but others' as well.

In the outer room, both sides patiently waited. Bill appeared confident as he normally did. In the bathroom, I ran into Bill's mother and niece. They ignored me. I take after my dad, and I'm always looking for opportunity to be friendly. But there was no opportunity for friendliness here.

I would be last to speak in my own defense, further testing my faith. First up were Bill and his family. Many people were there in his defense—his mother, preacher, teachers from the kids' daycare. But what did any of them know about me really? They were there to raise him up, as was my support team for me. Although there were some things Bill's family didn't know about him—like that we both had incurred sleepless nights of partying—these tidbits were now irrelevant. The focus was on what he was doing now, which was stepping up and being a father to Jayden and Annie. And that's okay. If it's God's will, then so be it. It's all about what's best for the children. I prayed for God's will to be done, and this meant a lot. I only hoped that their hearts and minds could have received my spoken words. Perhaps Bill and his family did, but by the way they still treat me, I doubt it. From the start, however, Judge Martin was not on my side.

Bill and his family talked of all my drunken escapades. Deliberately, of course. But what if they had been better educated about addiction? Would that have made a difference? I sat uncomfortably at the table with our new attorney, Mr. Ewey. He was precise and defended me as best he knew how. I recall him preparing me beforehand in a precourt meeting. He kept saying, "Now, Alisa, you have got to quit straying from the subject." This was hard for me. I wanted to be able to justify my answers, it was difficult for me to just say yes or no. I wanted to explain myself in detail. But in a setting where I was already guilty, it did not matter who my attorney was or what I said. They heard only what they wanted to hear. After all, they held the power, or so they thought. The prosecutors and judge were as cold as ice to me, offering no leeway. Family members listened quietly in the back while everything was laid out on the line. Those who were not in the courtroom had their ears pressed against the back door, waiting their turn to speak. The event played out like a scary movie. I felt bad for my family, and I was once again ashamed. Of course, they knew my past, but hearing such graphic details firsthand must have been difficult.

So, I sat there patiently praying, with my one-year gold-medallion chip tightly clutched in my left hand. This chip was a reminder of hope and of all that I had been through. No matter what the end result of this court date, I could move on as I had done before. Life is truly all about the journey. In the journey, you learn to dance when there is no music and sing when there are no songs. Only then do you realize what your true potential is.

One person after another took the stand to support Bill. Even his preacher took the stand. Bill had never gone to church before, but it was convenient now. If anything, I hope that this experience introduces him to God. Only God knows. I can't tell by talking to him. The day dragged on, past four o'clock. It was now our turn to take the stand. But it would have to wait until tomorrow. The big day had been another disappointment. Despite the time, however, Judge Martin made room for the first speaker on my behalf. Mr. Scott Van Krevelen.

Scott, a busy man taking care of addicts day in and day out, had prior obligations for the next day. He couldn't come back another day. So they let him speak. I was hopeful with this witness because of Scott's credentials and history. Scott is a former policeman and former OU football player. He is the director of Van's House, and he is a recovering alcoholic. He has long since closed the door on his battered past and created a beautiful ministry to help others. We were both grateful to find the trail of everlasting life, so we each closed the doors on the old life. And now, with twenty-eight years of sobriety, he was a living, breathing testimony that it could be done—and I could certainly relate to that. But it didn't mean that others would do the same.

Scott testified how Dusty and I had made it through the program successfully and that I had even worked on my college courses while in the girls' house. He pointed out that I had obtained my degree in business and management shortly after graduating from Van's House. I was proud of Scott and thankful he was there for me in a way that no one ever had been before. I will be forever grateful. No matter if the judge didn't see it, we had a pact. A band of God's eternal love. But the judge viewed us differently. He was also a drug-court judge, and I was just another failed project.

The brilliant, shining sun had brightened our house that morning, just as beautiful as always. That's the thing about planet Earth. Catastrophic events seem to place a hold on our lives day after day, but the sun shines anyway. The thunder keeps on rolling. It's a continuous cycle that has no end. But when it's storming, there is always hope for a better day. The events of this cold world are what we make of them. We can chose to sulk in them or choose to keep moving. No matter what happened, I told myself, I would choose to keep moving. I had come too far; I had run on a dead-end path for too long. I had now staked my claim to sobriety, and I wanted the world to know it. I wanted to shout, "You can overcome this disease! Look at me! I did it!" The problem was that these criticizers had not walked in my unique journey and had not seen the things that I had seen. Unless their hearts were softened, unless they knew of forgiveness, we wouldn't see eye to eye. They would continue to judge me as just an addict and not an overcomer. But

God saw my journey before it ever started, and He knows the end of my story. I am just thankful I was receptive to the call.

The hearing proceeded with another glorious day bestowed upon us. Hesitant but hopeful. At this point anything could happen. I played the scene from the day before over and over in my head—Bill on the stand, gazing my way and exposing his rage toward me. His mother took the stand judgingly. She said I must have been drinking, that my speech was slurred, and that all she could hear was the baby crying in the background. But in my mind, true or not, I was redeemed. But not all are keen to the view of the Most High. Most people are ruptured by the hard, cruel world.

There was proof that Bill was not perfect. He admitted he was going to counseling for anger issues. However, this proceeding concerned what would be best for the children. Not who but what. An award of full custody was not supposed to mean one parent was better than the other. This was not a game. We are all God's children. And God doesn't want partial custody. So it should be with our children. Even if one parent is ordered partial custody, the kids should receive full-time benefits. From both parents.

On the second day, boldly stepping one by one into the spacious marble room, my support line took the stand. During questioning, Dad admitted he had become intolerant of my actions. Too many times, I had failed him. But with all that, he was now confident I would remain sober. He loved his little girl and believed the best would shine through. He had not given up, and his faith was finally paying off. Aunt Linda spoke the same language. And then there was Dusty's ex-wife Emily, who testified on my behalf that she trusts me with her daughter Addi, and that she was thankful Addi had me in her life. Most exes are resentful toward the "other woman," but Emily was different. I was grateful for her. For all of them. After all I had done, my family still believed in me.

Clearly, I still had my opposing forces, but God had positioned the right people in my life to help erase the past and paint a newer, better picture. These were the ones I chose to listen to, and the colors of my new life blended beautifully. Although I could not paint like my mother, I was now part of her work. I was thankful for Van's House and all the wonderful people who had held onto the rope when it would have been easier to let go. Addicts can recover. All they need is faith, hope, encouragement, and love—a requirement for anyone who hopes for peace and joy.

God places people and things in our lives, and we can either accept them or not. I shot for acceptance and hit right on target. The trick was to keep on believing in the people who believed in me. But at this moment, Judge Martin was not one of these people. And this is one of the consequences I had to face because of my wrong decisions.

At last, it was my turn to speak. Exhausted from the anticipation, I approached the podium and raised my right hand. Yes, I agreed to tell the truth. Everything had been laid out on the table; I feared no contest. I only wanted to glorify the Maker and reveal a story of redemption. Although this might not get my children back, I was hopeful that God, at least, could be glorified. This was about placing Jayden and

Annie in the best home, yes. But there was a greater purpose. Could anyone see it? Do you see it now?

A brief recess, and the time had come. The grand finale, and Judge Martin cut to the chase. His mind had already been made up. Immediately, the attack began. This is a story all too familiar from my past. Despair had no room in my present life, but it was certainly trying to push its way through.

"I bet you don't even know your sponsor's number," he carelessly remarked. My mouth just remained open, no words came out. But in my head, I solemnly replied *585-858-8852.*

Then he proceeded to go on about how he was also head of the drug-court program in Ponca City and he knew all about this kind of stuff. "I'll bet you, I have people in my drug court that have made it thirty days and are probably more sober than you!"

Wow! Nothing like stabbing you in the gut when you've been knocked down. This was painful! I didn't hear any more. My selective hearing kicked. I had heard all I was going to hear. And I knew the answer to this long-awaited moment. My heart sank. Though outwardly I was calm, these words stung my heart and pierced open its wounds. Yet through all this, I heard the words of everlasting life. That although I would not get full custody of my children back, I would never lose them. I was their mother. God had chosen me for this. I had been given another chance. Forgiven. That was me. No longer measurable by man, God's strength would forever seep through me and He would forever seek me out as He always has.

Across the hall, that familiar grim smile crossed Bill's face. He knew he'd had this from the beginning, and so did the judge. He didn't like to lose, and the ball was in his court now. But that's not what this was about. This was about God's will. And according to that, I was not a loser. This was God's game. And He never fails.

Prosecutors claimed that Jayden and Annie were better off now in Bill's permanent custody. But I continued to struggle to even be informed of events such as school plays and conferences. It was as though I was nonexistent. True, Bill owed me nothing. But we could still work together for the good of the children, couldn't we? Although I may not understand it, I will never give up on being God's best for today and leaving tomorrow in His mighty hands.

I trust that God is always watching over my children and that I am forever with them in their hearts. Although I am not always with them physically, I am with them. And that will never change. I pray for them every day that they may have the best. And when they are with Dusty and me, we do our best to make the time count.

Our small increments of time together make our visits special. I am grateful for this time, because we all know it could have been worse. Now they can have the best from both sides. The timing just wasn't right on this one. There was more preparation on my part to be done. For example, Dusty and I were not married yet. But God's timing is never wrong. And the time for holy matrimony would come.

CHAPTER 9

Little Blessings

In the Bible, we are taught that God is a forgiving God (Matthew 6:14), that He has a plan to prosper us and not to harm us, to give us hope and a future (Jeremiah 29:11), and if we seek Him with all our hearts, we shall find Him (Jeremiah 29:13). The world tried its best to convince me otherwise. In my addiction, I did not believe I was worthy of God's love, and I surely didn't believe I had a future. And not once did I imagine God blessing me with another child. But this proved the point exactly. I was forgiven. Redeemed. And I was worthy, despite the world's opinion. I had been believing the world for too long. It was time for a fresh start.

L ife is one big rollercoaster with ups and downs and in-betweens. There are moments worth cherishing, and there are moments to be disregarded. We may think life is over at some particularly momentous event, but really that moment is just a stopping point. As that moment ends, a new one begins. What we do with each moment is really up to us. My new family from Van's House taught me to cherish life's gifted moments and leave the rest. So that's what I chose to do. I took what I wanted, and I left the rest. I anticipated the wake of a new day. Every day.

God was walking with me now. He had always been there, but I had chosen to walk away. I needed to discover who I really was, despite all the sin of the world and despite the alcohol that had held residence in my body for way too long. Through that desolate walk, through the endangered wilderness, I'd found an entanglement. I could not proceed until the path before me was untangled. But it was a tight knot. My fingers, small in comparison to the knot, struggled in vain. So I called out for help. Suddenly, the knot began to loosen. Slowly, but assuredly. And then, like that, it broke loose! Swinging into the air, I grabbed hold and held on tight. I now wanted to go a different route. A route not known to man. So I began my ascending climb upward into the sky. The sky truly was the limit.

This newfound journey was brighter, more beautiful than before. Before the alcohol clouded my way, I'd had a wider gaze. But now I had a much narrower path; it was clearer, and it was fulfilling. Much deeper. I wanted to invite more people to join me on this new, adventurous path. And then something unexpected occurred.

Knowing my past, I never expected God to give me another chance. But it was God's way of showing me how life continues on. One day, out of the blue, a long-forgotten feeling struck me by the wayside. Gut instinct? Something was different. I purchased the pregnancy test. And, yes, Dusty and I would be having a baby! I was surprised, but not really. A mix of emotion soon swept over me. Like a ripple effect, the rising sensation of excitement soon took precedence. Like ocean waves breaking onto the shore, life truly did move on.

As I held this new life inside me, my mind began to wonder and questions filled the air. But I was no longer engulfed by fear, so the feeling was one of excitement. I looked to my Father in heaven for the answers He had already given me but the world had taken away. Was I worthy of another child? Could I be a good mother? Despite my shameful, dried-up past, I was back from the dead. Not that I wasn't still a mother to Jayden and Annie, but I was now a weekend mommy, and I struggled with that fact for some time. Guilt, shame, you name it—these were my God-given children who needed their mom, and I had messed up. But my mistakes did not have to haunt me forever. Although I didn't know God's plan for my future, I knew that He was an awesome God, because look how far I had come already.

I never thought I could love another child as much as I loved Jayden and Annie. I was so caught up in trying to get my kids back that I never imagined that life could move on, and even be better than before. Our new baby boy, Braxton Lee, was born on November 29, 2012. He is a blessing for the whole family. Jayden, Annie, and Addi, proud of their new brother, beam with joyfulness at the sight of him. Braxton bears witness that life goes on. That love prevails. All the while, God remains on His throne.

I now had another go at it. Full-time. With two degrees fresh in hand, I first had another quest—to be a full-time mom to our new baby boy. Everything was lining up as it should be but there was one last vital ingredient to fully reside in God's will. Dusty and I needed to get married.

I have learned a new language—beautiful, unique in all its glory. The language of love. Brought to me once again by our Redeemer.

Our family has learned the true meaning of gratefulness. We've learned to overcome the bad and to appreciate the good that life has to offer. I have learned to take life by the horns as it comes stampeding toward me, trying to push me back into the past. But I possess a tight grip on the truth.

With God as my leader, I will never allow the bull of addiction to attack me again. There is too much at stake. As long as God remains my leader, I can confidently win this battle between heaven and hell.

Braxton, 10-months-old

Each morning I now wake up with anticipation, looking not for a drink, but to be a mother. I can continue on with the day, hopeful, looking into Braxton's beautiful, big, brown eyes, and receiving the confirmation of a life worth living. Not that this world is always great. We live in a treacherous society. But I have learned to make the best of it, and to be prepared for whatever trial may come because I know where I'm going. This is a far cry from three-and-a-half years ago.

I have the privilege of being a full-time mom again. Braxton and I dance and sing to music as the rhythm soothes our souls and we embrace the moment. We never miss a beat. The sounds of our happy voices are heard throughout the house and the music radiates the heavens—music to the angels' ears. Braxton loves to smile and laugh. He is a happy baby, unscathed by the evil of this world, and it is my job to keep it that way. He is indeed, a miracle, as all God's children are. This baby boy represents a new beginning for all, as people smile at his joyfulness. I am his hope for the future, and he is mine. The most joyful baby in the world keeps Dusty and I counting our blessings. No more remorse for the past. The slate is wiped clean. Jayden and Annie have their mommy back, and Dusty's daughter Addi has a new stepmom. We all have each other, with our heads rightfully attached. I can now be a better example and help lead them in God's footprints. In the end we can live together infinitely. That alone makes this experience worth it all.

CHAPTER 10

God's Promises Fulfilled

Because I didn't get my children back, I thought I failed miserably as a mother. But I was hugely mistaken. There is always a better plan with God. His is the best plan. Time took its course, and life traveled on. There was still more to be accomplished. I had every reason to move ahead, full force, to reach my highest potential. I now had a new, positive perspective on life. Gratefulness was a gift. This new beginning I'd been granted felt good. My new start did involve the kids, even though I wasn't granted full custody. My only regret is that I wanted to be involved in their school life—the plays, the back-to-school nights, and recreational activities. But the distance has put a damper on all that. Dusty and I thought it would be best if we made Enid our new home. Away from old people, places, and things. But temptation would be inevitable, no matter where we went. I'm the first to admit, addiction lurks in the most unlikely people. Even soccer moms and churchgoers. Despite the ramifications of all my sin, God promises that through Him, I may have everlasting life. And through Him, my purpose in life will be fulfilled. As long as I keep climbing.

J ayden and Annie were adjusting well to their new home in Ponca City and their new school nearby. Not that a home had never existed with me—I had provided a home at first, but its structure soon became torn by addiction. It was no safe haven. An addiction house never is. We now visited every other weekend. Progress from the random visits at McDonalds, that's for certain. But dropping them off never got any easier. My heart would ache as Annie stood in the doorway waving goodbye. A new week to survive, more days on end without Jayden and Annie. But with God's help, I coped. With all the obstacles I had overcome, I knew better than to sulk. After all, the kids were happy, and I was fortunate: I'd lived to tell. No more losing at this sorry game. I had rolled the dice too many times. Although my mind often drifted away in the cloud of *what ifs,* prayer quickly brought me closer to earth. Not that earth was a better place, but I knew I had to make the best of it. To set an example for the less fortunate who might not have heard of a man named Jesus, glorious in all His splendor.

I have many dreams for each of our children; Jayden, Annie, Addi, and Braxton. As they carry on with their everyday life, I pray they remember my face. Smiling, joyful in God's presence, I imagine holding their hands and giving them comfort in a cruel world. Assuring them that nothing in this world can detour them from the truth of an everlasting God.

That if their mom can overcome, so can they. I hope they have learned through me to never give up. And that I have never given up on them, and I never will.

My newfound sobriety inspired me to achieve more. So I began my next journey of attaining a master's degree. Although I was still unsure of what my future held, I felt the tug to go for it. I knew that I could do all things through Christ, who strengthens me. If I could believe it, I could achieve it. What did I have to offer to the world? There were now numerous possibilities. My life was on the open road, and God was the driver. Next stop: I decided to write a book sharing my story with others. But this journey came to a halt for a while. I had more to add to my story; there were a couple more chapters yet to be revealed. My new life soon played them out with happy endings. But there will never really be an ending to my story. Our story. Because God's words now grace the pages. And I desire to share them with others.

So I enrolled in an online master's program for organizational leadership, with the hope of one day running my own show. What kind of show would I be presenting? I didn't know yet, but I studied diligently, enjoying my brain's new capacity to the fullest extent. Every new adventure was a sacred quest. For every missed opportunity from my past, news ones appeared. I had a lot of catching up to do, so I got busy.

I got a job as an intern for the City of Enid. I was helping the community, reaching out to others. Yes, the government hired an old addict like me. I enjoyed helping manage a youth program and bringing opportunity to our youngsters. I began planting seeds I'd never known existed. Previously, there had been no seeds to plant. Our world needs much more of this awareness. Every event in life has a purpose. Each is connected, one after the other. A chain of events. This time, the linkages were strong, hardened by lessons learned. Built strong by the Truth.

It was time for another graduation. This time with my master's degree. With my heart and mind now tightly intact, there were no more screeching halts. I could now ride in the fast lane, guilt free! But I would not speed. I would abide by the rules. Dusty and I agreed to travel the ten hours to Illinois so I could walk across that stage. It was a fun trip and a special occasion. I wished Jayden, Annie, and Addi could have made it. To see their mom graduate with such honors would be inspiring for them. But they were well aware of my achievement. Jayden asked that I buy the graduation video so he could watch his mom graduate. That meant a lot. It meant that, no matter what events we miss out on, we can still find a way to share in those moments. Even the little things mean so much.

Then, there was more! I returned to the island life, this time under better circumstances. On July 3, 2013, Dusty and I got married on the beach at Montego Bay, Jamaica. The timing was now right, we'd completed our premarital counseling, and we were both ready to take the plunge. It was a perfect, sunlit day in Montego Bay as we said our "I do's" on the beach. This sacred day was the icing on the cake; we were finally in God's will.

Master's degree, baby, marriage, and the completion of this book. All within one year by the grace of God. I was redeemed.

I had acquired forgiveness, recovery, and God's grace. Freedom had never been sweeter. Although the road to this unique path seemed incomprehensible at first, looking back, it all makes perfect sense now. And it was all worth it. God followed through and continues to follow through with His plan. Just as He does with all of us. Trying to understand it all should have never been part of my goal. Instead, trust should forever reside in it.

Make no mistake, Dusty and I struggled in the beginning. We both had our share of brokenness. Relationships can be difficult enough without adding personal recovery from alcohol and drugs to the mix. Learning to put the past behind us and move on in relationship was a huge task. But we agreed to move forward together. We had our own struggles to work through, but we never gave up on each other. We kept God at the center, realizing we had to let go of self. We had to place it aside and look up to a loving God. We reminded each other of this at the most opportune times. Soon, we found a three-bedroom rental house not far from Dusty's work. Our choices were limited with our tainted backgrounds, so we were grateful to receive the call. Another one of God's handiworks made just for us.

We know now we should have been married from the start, because that is God's will. Dusty, a hard worker, remained solid at his job as a diesel mechanic. Later, we would become solid in our relationship. But this didn't occur while we were still living in sin. It occurred after. We worked hard for our children, for things we previously took for granted, like a simple walk with the kids or a visit to the park on a cool, autumn day.

Breakfast at our new, manmade marble table with room for the whole family. We started from scratch at our new home, and it was bittersweet. Our couch, a Rent-a-Center special, is cozy and spacious and is ours now. It certainly worked holding our family of six. Three rambunctious yet wonderful kids, a happy baby, and Dusty and me. Although three of the seats were often empty, we were grateful they got filled at all. Our life was now complete.

Our wedding day, July 3, 2013.

CHAPTER 11

A New Perspective

No one is perfect, although some may not care to admit this. Some people hide secrets, presenting themselves flawless on the surface. Worse, some are not aware of their transgressions at all! We are heavily judged by the world and by each other. Instead of helping our neighbors, we point fingers and gossip—but all the while we are the perpetrators lacking in wisdom. Ideally, we should be making the world a better place together, helping one another, and most of all loving as Jesus would love. In my addiction, I was the one hiding the truth. I acted as if nothing were wrong and lived as the world would live. My prayer is that people will find true life before it's too late.

Though life has not always been easy, thankfully, I now have a new perspective. Why did I have to become an alcoholic? Why couldn't I just drink one or two like the others? Why did I think I had to drink the whole twelve-pack instead? Why couldn't others just understand me? So many unanswered questions, not made for me to comprehend. But what I thoroughly understand is that I have been positively transformed by my past. I always had the desire to succeed, but then alcohol and drugs moved in. But God knew I would find the strength to make it out of that dark forest. So He would use me as a messenger to help others who had found their way to the darkness. If I hadn't gone there, I would not have learned to place my trust in God. But now I have to guide others out of the dark.

We live in a temporary garden called earth. God planted the seeds and watered them here. There were lots of thirsty plants here. And so He quenched our thirst. In this garden were other plants as well, already beginning to bloom. But one single creation was poisoned by an unknown substance. So for a while, the garden suffered. Darkness invaded it. The little plants that had started to grow began to struggle as well. The infected plant looked up for sunshine, but only found the rain. But with the rain, came growth. And suddenly, the sun began to shine, and the sad plant began to thrive. This so inspired the little plants and all the other surrounding ones that they looked for the sunshine, too. "Bring on the rain!" they cried. The garden flourished, filled with bright, exquisite, thriving flowers and plants formerly unknown to man. A true masterpiece was this garden. And so I decided I wanted to stay, and others did too. But they had to see me make it through to live to tell about it.

And such is life. We are in this garden, and we are each deeply impacted by one another. Many of us have become poisoned by sin, but if we look up, we can make it through the hurricane and come out better on the other side. The sun shines brighter than it did before. And our senses are more keen to enjoy the view.

I wouldn't wish this disease and the pain that goes with it on anyone. It is painful, devastating, and heartbreaking. But even if you're not an alcoholic or an addict, I know that you know that life can be painful. At times, excruciating. When I went to Van's House, I was one of the worst cases Scott and Sally had ever seen. Yet I made a total transition. So I want you to know that if I can do this, so can you. And if I am worthy of God's love after all the damage I caused to others and myself, so are you. You don't have to live as a prisoner to your past. Once you're plugged into God, you learn that what people think really doesn't matter. You learn that you are here to help them become more like Christ. Because in the end, that's all that matters. I would not have been able to fully comprehend this concept without having gone through all my misery and shame. Without having been an addict, I would not have truly known God. For that, I am forever obliged.

Not everyone who drinks in an alcoholic. But there are many out there who are certainly pushing the envelope! As I stand now in hindsight—on the outside looking in—I see the demons of addiction spreading like unruly waves in a sea of turbulence. Ever more often, we hear of people dying from overdoses, of incarceration because of actions taken while under the influence, of alcohol-related vehicular accidents. We see families being ripped apart, divorces, babies addicted because of their mothers, and children being taken away from their mothers and fathers. All from this ugly disease of addiction to alcohol and drugs. I speak not from a master's degree in addiction; I am in another field of study. I speak from experience, the best of its kind.

Perhaps there are some people who are in denial that they even have a problem to begin with. This further complicates matters. And there are those who are unaware of the extent of their addictions. I was one of those. I went on drinking and partying like everyone else because I thought I would get over that phase. But, sadly, I was wrong. Oftentimes it's hard to identify an alcoholic because drinking is so socially acceptable. There at the end, it was pretty obvious my life had spiraled out of control. But no one knew what to do with me. That is why I'm here to tell you—if you or your loved one or anyone else you know is in trouble from this disease, get help now.

Living in Van's House, I watched countless men and women come and go. Making it one whole year is too high a price for many. For some, a week is difficult enough. And these are the cases that want to be there. There are also those that are court-ordered, and the success rate for them is minimal to none. That is, until they come to the realization that they have a problem, and they desire change.

The judge who ordered custody of Jayden and Annie to their father had it all wrong. He had put me in a category with his many former drug-court prospects that had failed. For a long while, I held onto a struggling resentment toward this man that didn't know me because of his inaccurate judgment. I had worked very hard to get clean. But I have since let go of that resentment, and I have made a pact with myself that I will continue to prove the critics wrong and help them while I'm at it. That's the whole point of my overcoming my addiction—to show that God redeems! And no one can take that truth away!

I pray that standing up boldly to share my story just might help you to face your own demons. To stand up to whatever it is you need to deal with. Think positively and go for it! Life is short, and time is precious. Who knows, we may be raptured up tomorrow—a constant reminder to myself and to others to keep growing in Christ and sharing our knowledge with those around us. I know I wasted many years because of my infatuation with alcohol and drugs. Well, it's time I pulled the plug. I've got a decade to make up for! Isn't it ironic that, normally I am a private person, yet this is one of the most revealing accounts a person could share about themselves. And, hey, I love to write, so God made it count. After all, He does know best.

And so, we come to the end of my story. Which is really just the launch of the next chapter in my life.

For all the terrible decisions I made because of alcohol, I am forgiven. For all the times I drank and drove, I am forgiven. For the times I neglected my children…forgiven. For all the worry and tears I caused…forgiven. God has delivered me from my addiction to alcohol and drugs. I am no longer branded and shamed by my past. The same that holds true for me, can hold true for you as well.

My new perspective says I am blessed to have been stricken by this illness. Now I can truly live—live to be my very best. I can appreciate the break of a new day each morning and fall of the night at dusk, peacefully assured the sun will rise again because I am redeemed. Forgiven. Set free.

Even as I reflect on my loss of full custody of Jayden and Annie, I am enlightened with the certainty that I can now be a better mother and appreciate even the smallest moments. I am confident that will never go away. And our family is so thankful to have Braxton as part of our new lives. A sweet, little blessing I never thought I was worthy of. But there's where I was wrong again. God always knew the person I was meant to be and that I would become in the end. I am a loving Christian mother who loves her children dearly. All the other stuff was just a learning experience. One which I passed, by the way, making the grade yet again.

For all of these things, I am blessed. My addiction granted me new life and gave new life. I am fortunate that I am redeemed and that freedom has never been sweeter. My prayer is that you may find that same freedom from bondage that I did.

If you or a loved one needs help with alcohol or drugs, Scott and Sally Van Krevelen from Van's House are here to help! Give them a call at 580-233-6070 or visit them at www.vanshouse.com